Naval Ship Models of World War II

Naval Ship Models
of World War II
in 1/1250 and 1/1200 Scales

Enhancements, Conversions & Scratch Building

Robert K Liu

Seaforth
PUBLISHING

Title page: AA ships, top to bottom, 1/1250 unless noted as 1/1200; only AA listed: Neptun cruiser *Maya* (16.4cm OAL), six twin 127mm, thirteen triple 25mm, two single 25mm. N1141B *Black Prince* anti-aircraft cruiser (12.7cm OAL), a modified *Dido*, stock, four twin 5.25in, three quad pom-poms, eight twin 20mm, one single 20mm. N1168 *Delhi* anti-aircraft cruiser (11.7cm OAL), stock, five 5in/38 calibre, two quad pom-poms, eight single 20mm. Framburg *Scylla* anti-aircraft cruiser (13.2cm OAL), 1/1200, die-cast, a *Dido* class equipped with four twin 4.5in main guns, two octuple pom-pom, poorly modelled. Superior *Isuzu* anti-aircraft cruiser (13.2cm OAL), 1/1200, completely modified by author, with three twin 127mm, eleven triple 25mm, one single 25mm. John Youngerman *San Diego* CLAA (13.7cm OAL), 1/1200, scratch-built, as in 1942, made in October 2011, eight twin 5in/38 calibre, three quad 40mm, eight single 20mm. John Youngerman Dutch *Jacob van Heemskerck* anti-aircraft cruiser (11.1cm OAL), 1/1200, made in April 2002, five twin 4in, one quad pom-pom, six single 20mm. HMS *Springbank* AA ship (10.7cm OAL, including rudder), four twin 4in, two quad pom-poms, two quad 0.50 MGs, scratch-built by author on hardwood hull and partial superstructure of stripped model by Miles Vaughn; original model was 1/1200, but is now 1/1250. Cap Aero Fulmar on catapult. HMCS *Prince Robert* AA ship (9.45cm OAL), five twin 4in, two quad pom-poms, six single 20mm. Argonaut 1292 *Tynwald* AA ship (8.0cm OAL), with repaired turrets, guns and masts, now with yards, jackstaffs and radar, four twin 4in, two quad pom-poms, two quad 0.50 MGs. Helge Fisher 36 *Medusa* floating AA battery (8.4cm OAL), a converted WWI warship, six 10.5cm, one 37mm, one quad 20mm, five single 20mm, with the 37mm and quad sited asymmetrically. When models are modified or scratch-built, work is by the author.

Copyright © Robert K Liu 2021

First published in Great Britain in 2021 by
Seaforth Publishing,
A division of Pen & Sword Books Ltd,
47 Church Street,
Barnsley S70 2AS
www.seaforthpublishing.com

British Library Cataloguing in Publication Data
A catalogue record for this book is available from the British Library

ISBN 978 1 5267 9391 1 (HARDBACK)
ISBN 978 1 5267 9392 8 (EPUB)
ISBN 978 1 5267 9393 5 (KINDLE)

Unless otherwise credited, all photographs are by the author.

Pen & Sword Books Limited incorporates the imprints of Atlas, Archaeology, Aviation, Discovery, Family History, Fiction, History, Maritime, Military, Military Classics, Politics, Select, Transport, True Crime, Air World, Frontline Publishing, Leo Cooper, Remember When, Seaforth Publishing, The Praetorian Press, Wharncliffe Local History, Wharncliffe Transport, Wharncliffe True Crime and White Owl

Typeset and designed by Stephen Dent
Printed and bound in India by Replika Press Pvt Ltd

CONTENTS

PREFACE AND ACKNOWLEDGEMENTS

While the collecting and modelling of small-scale naval ships is largely a solitary activity, having contact with fellow enthusiasts greatly amplifies one's enjoyment. In 2002, I re-established contact with an old graduate school friend, Alexander White III, who I found out was also a small ship model collector. Between then and his death in 2013, I visited him over 100 times, to exchange ship/aircraft models and bring back his models to enhance and/or repair, even though he lived over a hundred miles away. Helping him to collect and improve his French Navy collection was also the impetus for me to record in greater detail what I did in my workshop, and to improve and develop my own modelling skills. Early on, most of my experience had not been shared with anyone except possibly ship model dealers, the earliest being Nathan R. Preston in the late 1990s-2000s, as well as the likes of Bill Grunner, Peter Wiedling, George Elder, Bill Werner and Chris Daley. George Elder, former owner of Morning Sunshine Models, has always offered good advice, support and friendship. I am grateful that Chris Daley, of 1250ships.com, often hosted my recent naval ship model blogs. Late in this book project, Bill Werner passed to me a hard-to-obtain model from his well-curated, nearly 4,000 strong, ship model collection. I had wanted to include a British-built escort carrier in the chapter on aircraft carriers and posted on 1250 Scale for a *Vindex* or sister ship. Werner offered a Hai *Pretoria Castle*. Because of conflicting information on her armament, I asked him to describe the AA on the Sea Vee *Pretoria Castle* model, as well as asking Sean Pritchard, the maker, about his sources. Thus I was able to correct and enhance the Hai model to a higher standard of accuracy, an excellent example of the type of generous help usually offered in the miniature ship model community.

I especially thank Peter Wiedling for the great value of his comprehensive warship and merchant vessel 'Ship Registers' (see bibliography), important aids to collecting and documentation. Equally helpful has been Kevin Holmes' series of 'Waterline Guides', available as free PDFs to download, that are informative, well-illustrated and useful when trying to identify ship models or producers. The sammelhafen.de or Olivers Welt website with its illustrated checklist of ship models continues to be an invaluable research tool, especially in deciphering ship types and models, and is being constantly updated. I thank Nate Rind of Antheil Booksellers for his quick and reliable service in supplying unusual and useful naval and other military publications, vital to being an accurate and knowledgeable modelmaker.

David Gregory of PT Dockyard was helpful with images and literature for many small ship types, as was his website with its useful links. Over twenty years ago, my friend Stephen Myhre, a carver from New Zealand, gave me some hand-made carving tools; these continue to be useful for carving the plastic, lead and tin alloys of small-scale ship and plane models. I thank Ulrich (Rick) Rudofsky for sharing his knowledge, expertise, observations on casting and great photographs of ship models and ship model related events. The late Jacqueline Ruyak and Nancy Ukai Russel have my gratitude for translating titles and charts from Japanese naval publications. I thank Mike Meyer, whom I met at a Society of Miniature Ship

Collectors (SMSC) gathering, for directing me to a Japanese website with good, scarce information on Japanese *marus*, gunboats and other such auxiliaries converted from merchant ships.

As I began to write about miniature ship models and then publish my own small books on this topic, I established contact with Alberto Mussino, a talented model-maker and editor for the now defunct Italian *Waterline International*, as well as more actively with Elder and Werner, both supportive of my writing and of our community of ship model collectors.

At American model ship dealer Chris Daley's 2006 meeting of 1/1250 model collectors in Claremont, I was able to meet a number of other collectors from California. In the 2007 northern California open house at Paul Jacobs, I saw his breath-taking model ship collection, covered in part in his 2008 book, as well as meeting more US collectors. At this event and the previous day, when Daley and Jacobs organised a sale of 1/1250 ship models in the No.2 hold of the WWII 'Liberty' ship SS *Jeremiah O'Brien* (one of two operational 'Liberty' ships in the world), I was able to meet and speak with the principals of leading German producers Neptun/Navis and Rhenania. In 2009, the SMSC was formed, which lead to national and regional conferences, widening every collector's contacts, including European, and increased collecting opportunities. The May 2008 Collectors Meeting at the Maritime Industry Museum in Fort Schyuler, NY, had also been a great opportunity to exchange information with other American and foreign producers and collectors, as well as to purchase used, out-of-production models, from Jim Angelis, Chris Daley and John A. Olsen, who has been a great source of Förde models, now out of production but only sold direct to collectors in the past.

Along with the formation of SMSC, the Internet opened most of the world to us, especially via the 1250 Scale and Dockside message boards, respectively based in the United States and the United Kingdom, as well as Münchner Rundbrief, which requires German language skills. Through these and other online forums, I have made many friendships, as our small community is usually very generous with on-line requests for help.

As with any specialised collecting field, the sources for buying and trading models and relevant publications are crucial for growing both one's collection and one's knowledge. Despite the Internet giving greatly improved access to sources of models and of information, the personal relationships that are formed during such transactions are what provide a great deal of the satisfaction. As Paul Jacobs discusses in his 2008 book on the collecting of miniature ship models, the Internet has played a large role in the expansion of interest in 1/1200-1/1250 ship models and made exchange of information and acquisition of models easier, but the beneficial effects of meeting face to face with collectors and dealers is immeasurable, especially in the US, where such opportunities are scarce, with only a few regional meetings plus a large annual conference, either on one coast or the other, or in the middle of the country.

Since I publish on my collecting and model making, I use my experience as a magazine editor/publisher to translate my writings and photographs into publications. I am thankful to have the help of our graphic designers, especially our current design consultant, Stephanie Screiber, and my son Patrick Benesh-Liu, who has taught me so much about InDesign and PhotoShop, as well as being patient in having his heavy workload often interrupted. I am also fortunate in being a professional photographer and jeweller myself, with studios at the magazine office and at home. I have shot numerous film and digital images of miniature model ships and aircraft, usually with macro lenses and strobe lights that permit high resolution and great depth-of-field in the photographs. Large, clear images are essential to showing the details of ship and airplane models.

My intense interest in naval ships of WWII, including many other aspects of this war, is probably is due to my family history. I was born in Rome in 1938, when my father was Chinese ambassador to Mussolini's government; prior to that he was Chinese minister to Hitler's Germany and Austria. My sister Margaret was born in Berlin during that period. For the Chinese, the world-wide war started in the 1930s, so we returned to China when Japan joined the Axis powers. Our return voyage to Shanghai was on the Italian liner *Conte Verde*, one of four Lloyd Triestino ships that served as a lifeline for Jewish refugees fleeing from Austria and Germany to Shanghai. She also served as an exchange ship for interned diplomats and others. *Conte Verde* was in Shanghai when the Italians signed the armistice in 1943; to prevent seizure by the Japanese, the crew scuttled her. According to my sister Margaret, some of the crew then opened a fine Italian resturant in Shanghai, introducing sour cream to the Chinese.

Between 1938 and 1944 we lived in Japanese-occupied China, mostly in Shanghai. In late 1944 the city came under attack by US aircraft, prob-ably by B25s of the Fifth Airforce, although B24s also bombed our city. Shortly afterwards we left on a three-month journey from Shanghai to Kuomintang-controlled Chungking, the wartime capital, to join my father who was with the Nationalist government. We travelled by train, wheelbarrow, mule cart, on foot at night to cross enemy lines, were pulled on wooden sleds across the frozen Yellow River and, finally, by open US International cargo trucks. After VJ Day, most of the family flew to Nanking in a C47 troop carrier, landing at an airport full of surrendered Japanese warplanes. My late, oldest brother John flew back in the tail gunner's position of a Chinese B25, which must have been heaven for a teenager inter-ested in engineering.

In our temporary Shanghai home, I met a German boy with a large wooden box of metal naval recognition models, probably Wiking ships, my first exposure to such miniature vessels. In 1946 we left for the US with my mother and five siblings, on the recently disarmed USS *Marine*

Lynx (T-AP 194). With the Communist takeover in 1949, we did not return to China. In the late 1940s, my late mechanical engineer brother John began building 1/1200 balsa ship models with me, starting my lifelong interest, ongoing at the age of 83. I cherish his instilling my interest in all things mechanical and how to work with my hands. I now realise how much the Sino-Japanese War, WWII and the Communist revolution have impacted my life, fuelling my fascination with the implements of these wars and attempting to repli-cate them in miniature, as I have also modelled and written about armoured vehicles and aircraft of WWII.

While the activity of building miniature ship and aircraft models is a solitary task, I firmly believe it is beneficial to one's mind and body. Most members of this community are relatively elderly, so keeping one's mental and physical facil-ities healthy is vital. At the age of 83, I find I am a much better modelmaker than when I was younger, and am still advancing my skills. I have written elsewhere about how easy it is to lose the numerous small parts required for ship model building, especially if one's workspace floor is covered with a rug. While I still lose parts that required much time to make, I recently devised a technique that at least reduces loss. When I make serial parts such as gun turrets or mounts, it is done on a larger sprue, after which the finished armament is cut off with a sharp craft knife or a jeweller's saw. The kinetic energy generated by these actions almost always kicks the small, finished part some distance, often beyond recovery. Now, I place the sprue and knife in a large, clear plastic bag to carry out the cutting, trapping the tiny part within the bag.

In the References and Bibliography section, I have tried to include three broad categories: those that deal with naval/aviation technology and history, those on small scale ship model-making and about the miniature scale ship model commu-nity, and those that are primarily pictorial and a help to modellers of both ships and aircraft.

1

INTRODUCTION

While this is a book about enhancing, modifying and scratch-building small-scale naval ship models, how and why one makes changes to a model also depends upon the type of collection. Here I use destroyers and escorts as a very good way to have a collection that is diverse and offers many chances at improving the models. Handling small-scale ship models, seeing how various makers translated the prototype into a miniature and the different ways each manufacturer works, especially evident when comparing models of the same ship from different firms, is an experience that adds much to the pleasure and the knowledge base of the collector. The physicality of the model, especially the weight or heft of the metal, all add to the miniaturised reality of it. If one both knows and researches historical and/or technical information about the prototype, there is enhanced vicarious enjoyment of the model. This is a vastly different experience compared to that of many younger people, for whom the digital or electronic object now holds much more interest, perhaps because these devices can be made to interact, unlike the static miniature ship model, where imagination plays an important role. Yet those in the small-scale ship model community continue to be enthralled with such objects. Why?

Models, like jewellery, can be both art and history; in correspondence with Burkhard Schütt of Risawoleska, producer of very fine models, who trained as an architect, I remarked that his ship models, like many others, could be appreciated as art and could be regarded as an important historical document of our times. His print documentation of the firm's models are as well done as many art publications.

To me, an accurate model is both a historic artifact and a memorial to what that particular naval vessel accomplished, and to her crew who enabled such accomplishments. I think combining modelmaking, research, writing, photography and printing is a very natural and rewarding way of working with one's mind and hands. Such activities enhance one's mental and physical life, and contribute to a sense of achievement and purpose. When I began in 2009 to work on the model ship collection of my late friend and collector Alex White, I made myself improve and innovate. He was mostly housebound, and derived much pleasure in looking at and actually handling his models, especially the French portion of his collection, for he had a deep and scholarly interest in the French Navy.

The worldwide community of people who collect and make naval ship models in 1/1250 and 1/1200 scales is small, concentrated in the UK, Western Europe, especially Germany, and the United States, with apparently a few outliers in Australia and Asia. There is a close correlation between the numbers of ship model collectors and the history of that country's navy, especially with regards to their warships that participated in WWI and WWII. Therefore, I feel that surviving WWII identification models and models derived from them form a firm basis for current collectors/modellers. So in this chapter I show a number of real wartime ID models and the exciting acquisition by Paul Jacobs of his rare 75-year-old set of Japanese ID models. Other similar Japanese ID models of later date with different paint schemes have been found in caves on the island of Okinawa and one set sold at

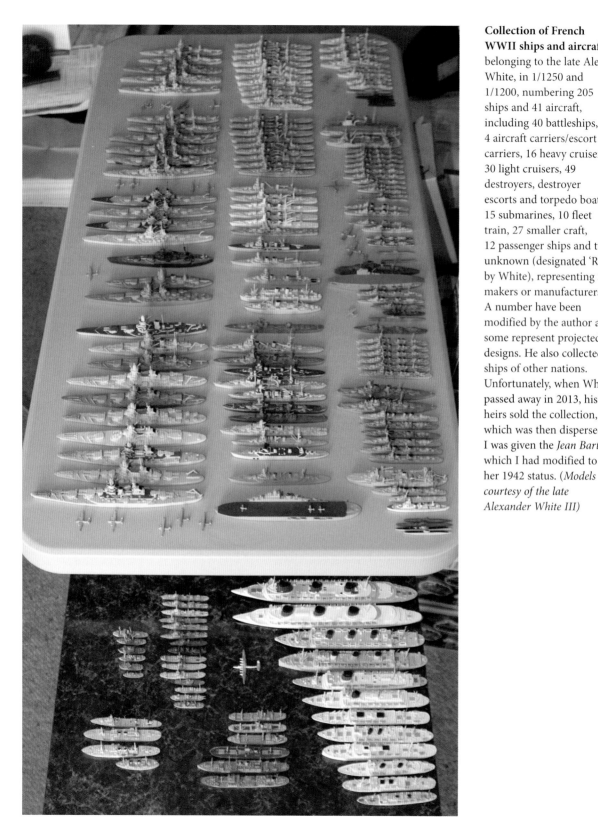

Collection of French WWII ships and aircraft belonging to the late Alex White, in 1/1250 and 1/1200, numbering 205 ships and 41 aircraft, including 40 battleships, 4 aircraft carriers/escort carriers, 16 heavy cruisers, 30 light cruisers, 49 destroyers, destroyer escorts and torpedo boats, 15 submarines, 10 fleet train, 27 smaller craft, 12 passenger ships and two unknown (designated 'RF' by White), representing 36 makers or manufacturers. A number have been modified by the author and some represent projected designs. He also collected ships of other nations. Unfortunately, when White passed away in 2013, his heirs sold the collection, which was then dispersed. I was given the *Jean Bart* which I had modified to her 1942 status. (*Models courtesy of the late Alexander White III*)

auction at Bonhams in 2019 for more than £9,000.

While there are well-known collectors, such as those behind the Tamm collection, no one has received as much attention regarding their collection as Norman Bel Geddes, one of America's most famous designers in the fields of art, architecture, consumer goods and theatrecraft. Adept at making large dioramas, he had an intense interest in long-lasting and complex wargames, including naval ones. In the course of seven years, probably in the late 1930s–early 1940s, employing a staff of jewellers, he supposedly built a collection of 1,700 naval ships, from silver or brass, in 1/1200 scale.

These were used in recreating WWII battles, meticulously lit and photographed in big studios. Bel Geddes had a show of his war-related dioramas/models at the Museum of Modern Art, New York, and was featured in *Life* magazine and *Popular Science*, two enormously popular and widely-read publications of the 1940s. His battle recreations also appeared in armed services journals. Part of his archive is now at the University of Texas, Austin, along with a few of the models. However, no one with sufficient knowledge has studied them to determine if they were scratch-built by Bel Geddes' staff, were wartime ID models produced by other firms, or a mix. Photos of his

Allied and Axis destroyers, *from top to bottom*: Neptun French *Magador*, Neptun US *Sumner*, Optatus British 'U' class, Neptun German *Z25*, Optatus Japanese *Nowaki* and Neptun Italian 'Soldati'. 8.5 to 11.0cm overall length. From this angle the bows, sterns and hulls, as well as the superstructures and guns, are shown well. German ships often look sprightly, due to the bright yellow of their life rafts, while on Allied ships these items usually blend with ship colours. The *Sumner* model has added radar, while the 'Soldati' could benefit from yards being added to the masts. British destroyers were more usually intricately camouflaged, although Japanese ones were not. The 'Soldati's style of dazzle camouflage was being used on all Italian warships by 1942.

Inspiration for a new project. When my son Patrick gave me a beautiful Neptun *Currituck* AV7, 1946, it offered an opportunity to enhance the used Superior *Curtiss*, which may take an appreciable amount of work to improve. Note how the PBM Mariner and Catalina enhance the image.

Allied and Axis destroyers, *from top to bottom*: Optatus Japanese *Nowaki*, Neptun German *Z25*, Neptun French *Magador* (note cruciform yards and aerial spreaders on second funnel); Neptun French *Le Terrible* and Neptun US *Sumner*. 9.2 to 11.0cm overall length. Even though two different producers made these models, the wood interior colours of the lifeboats are remarkably similar. These are models that have been so well made that there is no need to enhance them, other than the fact that sometimes yards are lacking.

British 'Hunt' class destroyers: *from left to right.* Clydeside, Wiking 'Hunt II', Framburg 'Hunt', Superior 'Hunt', Argonaut 'Hunts' *Brissenden, Grove*, '37' [identity uncertain], Figurehead 'Hunt' with bow 6pdr, Neptun 'Hunt III' and *Liddesdale* with bow 6pdr. 6.9 to 7.4cm overall length. Some have been slightly reworked, others are stock. The Framburg model dates from the 1940s, while the newest represent products of the 2000s, showing how much masters have improved and casting has changed in these decades. Framburg is die-cast, Wiking is plastic injection, Clydeside probably spin-cast while most German producers used silicon moulds. This little array of models is essentially a history of the small-scale ship model industry.

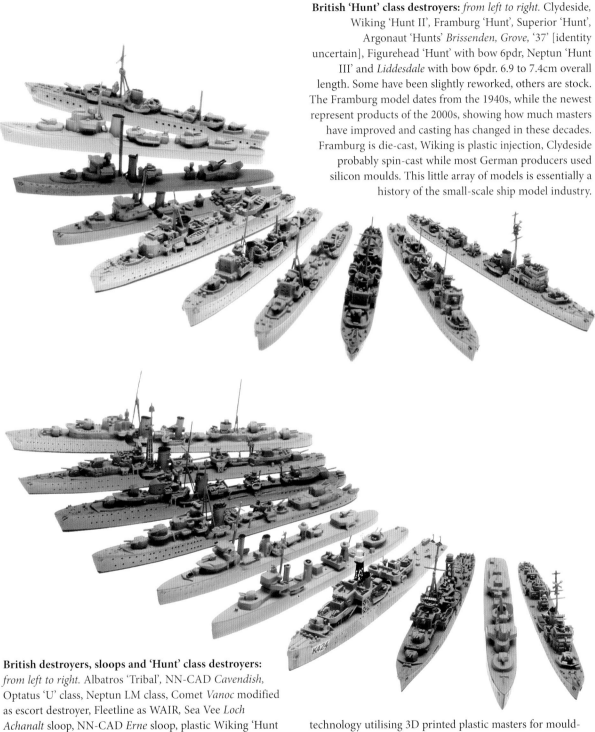

British destroyers, sloops and 'Hunt' class destroyers: *from left to right.* Albatros 'Tribal', NN-CAD *Cavendish*, Optatus 'U' class, Neptun LM class, Comet *Vanoc* modified as escort destroyer, Fleetline as WAIR, Sea Vee *Loch Achanalt* sloop, NN-CAD *Erne* sloop, plastic Wiking 'Hunt II' and Neptun *Liddesdale* 'Hunt II' in 1942 rig, with HF/DF antenna on foremast. 6.9 to 9.1cm overall length. The Sea Vee sloop is beautifully made, with extremely accurate and delicate photo-etch, while NN-CAD represents the latest technology utilising 3D printed plastic masters for mould-making. The Comet and Fleetline models have been extensively modified, the others are stock. Again, these models cover from post-WWII to today, illustrating how finely made such models are now.

Italian destroyers/escorts:
from top to bottom: Copy *Da Mosta*,
Neptun 'Soldati', Neptun *Freccia*, Neptun
Lampo, Albatros *Intrepido*, Neptun
Ciclione, Albatros *Ariete*, Copy *Castore*,
Neptun *La Masa* and Neptun *Gagriano*.
5.5 to 8.6cm overall length. Many Italian
destroyers and smaller escorts were
rather lightly armed, with guns set very
close together, but often with attractive
lines. The heaviest armed were only
comparable to the British 'Hunts', while
some Italian escorts carried only one or
two main-battery guns, with 37mm,
20mm AA or 13mm AA.

carriers show aircraft on deck; such aircraft were not commercially available.

In 2019, Chris Daley of 1250 ships.com, the largest dealer of 1/1250 and 1/1200 scale models in the US, conducted an online survey through his website. Of the respondents, approximately 75 per cent enjoy naval history, and 80 per cent collect warship models, predominately those from the period 1919–45. Almost 100 per cent of respondents were males, mostly 60 or older, with up to 45 per cent having bachelor and/or graduate degrees. From my own acquaintance with this worldwide group, I know that many are professionals. The survey also revealed that the three main ship model message boards, 1250 Scale Forum (US), Dockside (UK) and Münchner Rundbrief (Germany) are visited by between 15 per cent and 70 per cent, often daily. Most of the expert collectors/dealers who I asked believe

that there are around 3,000-5,000 collectors, if not all very active.

Producers of small ship models during the time period of the survey have been documented by Paul Jacobs in *Miniature Ship Models. A History and Collector's Guide* (2008), in Kevin Holmes' many illustrated 'Waterline Guides' (articles in British model magazines, also available as downloadable PDF files) and George H Elder's comprehensive MS Excel file of producers, major and minor. This 2016 list documented 427 makers of small-scale ship models, with the majority from Germany and the UK, though with a total of seventeen countries represented. In July 2019, an extensive online thread developed on the 1250 Scale Forum about those who produced hand-made models; Doug Knowlton of Rio Grande Models listed thirty-one makers of wooden ship models, demonstrating the value of such message

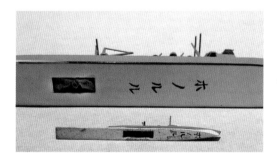

Extremely rare Japanese ID ship model sets from the 1940s: *from left to right, top to bottom:* two drawers of 1/1000 and 1/5000 wood/metal models of American ships recently acquired by Paul Jacobs, collector, model maker/producer and author. Adjacent is a drawer with British recognition models that come with the American set, as well as a British set with *Eagle* and *Glorious* (the latter had been sunk by time this set, numbered 24, was made in 1941, as deduced by Jacobs). A friend of Jacobs has a British set numbered 78, so a fair number of sets seem to have been made. Jacobs's set was 'liberated' by a US sailor who was serving in Japan after the end of the war. Note that all the models are on wooden plinths, each with a painted bow wave; metal castings fit into the bottom to hold them in place in wooden drawers. Each has sumi ink calligraphic label on bottom of wood hull. *Brooklyn* and *Yorktown*; 1/1000 = 22.9cm, 1/5000 = 5.0cm. These models are made to a good standard, at least as well as the Admiralty model of the French light cruiser *La Galisonniere*. Note that decks are painted on this ID model. (*All photographs courtesy of Paul Jacobs, except French light cruiser courtesy of the late Alexander White III*)

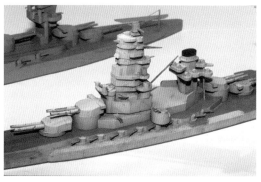

WWII recognition models: *from left to right, top to bottom*: Navy Memorial Museum, Navy Yard, D.C. Identification display of cased 1/1200 recognition model sets, with 1/200 and 1/300 scale ones in front; grey drawers contain unpainted metal 1/2000 and 1/5000 ship model sets. Various wartime Navy publications in front. Rare Japanese battleship *Ise*, handmade wood/metal 1/500 model at the Maritime Museum of San Diego, one of nineteen found at Kure Navy base in September 1945. Display case on board SS *Victory Lane*, showing wood/metal ID models of WWII (*Warspite*, *Hood* and *Barham* in 1/1200). I am unable to determine if these are made by Boucher, by Bassett Lowke, or are Admiralty models. Adjacent image shows ONI recognition manual and cast metal 1/1200 naval models made by US manufacturers, although I am unable to determine whether these are by Comet, Framburg, or someone else.

Neptun *Sumner* destroyer vs Paper Lab TH002 *Winslow* DD 359: examples of current German silicon mould-produced metal model and first generation 3D rapid prototype manufacturing, the latter by Darius Lipinski of Canada, who now uses this process to make masters for metal casting by German producers. 9.3 to 9.5cm overall length. The resin model is very light and fragile. Many 3D modellers now produce their work through Shapeways, a Dutch firm with a branch in New York City, although some of the best 3D printed ship models come from individual European producers.

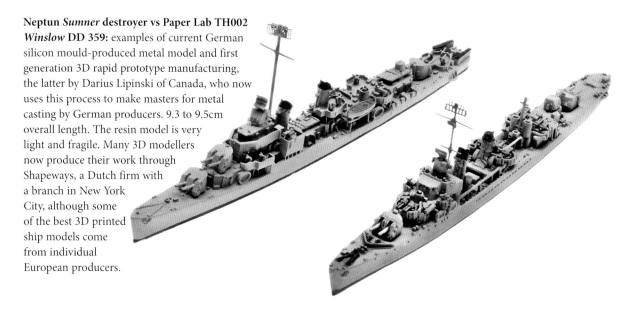

boards for information otherwise difficult to access.

In fact, information or knowledge about naval technology, history and how to work with small tools are vital to becoming a good modelmaker. When I first started collecting WWII naval ship models, I knew too little to judge whether a model was accurate or not, and whether it needed work. Thus, guidance from an experienced collector can help a novice, as can getting hold of

perhaps the most important element, good quality publications about naval ships. One needs to acquire those books that are well illustrated, those that provide technical information, and those that contain operational histories of vessels. My military library numbers more than 500 volumes, more than my model collection. These days I also start each project with an Internet search on the subject.

It helped that my late engineer brother John

Radar picket group of late Pacific war, comprising destroyers, LSM(R) and LCS(L)s, represented here by 1/1200 Clydeside *Fletcher* (five 5in/38, one twin 40mm, ten 20mm) cleaned up and enhanced, with radar added; Neptun *Sumner* (three twin 5in/38, two quad 40mm, two twin 40mm, eight 20mm) was stock except for addition of radar; Figurehead LSM(R) was cleaned up and detailed, with camouflage; Neptun LCS(L) stock and modified by author to three twin 40mm, with radar/yard added, four 20mm barrels replaced and with camouflage scheme. These two Landing Craft Support, Large, known collectively as 'Mighty Midgets', swapped their bow gun for another twin 40mm, giving them

three such twin 40mm and six 20mm. Destroyers were the most numerous radar pickets at Okinawa, with 57 *Fletchers* and 22 *Sumners*, while 11 LSM(R)s and 88 LCS(L)s also served as such. The Landing Ship Medium (Rocket) had an inadequate defensive armament and they should not have served in this battle, but they were needed. This horrendous battle against overwhelming numbers of *kamikaze* and regular Japanese aircraft has been well documented elsewhere, but to give one example, *Laffey*, a *Sumner* class destroyer, was attacked off Okinawa by 22 planes, shot down 9 but was struck by 7 *kamikazes*. Of the destroyers serving in the battle, 42 out of 101 ships were sunk or damaged.

Small boats/ships of the US Navy in the SW Pacific, where destroyers and smaller vessels did yeoman work. Collecting ship models by theatre of action is a meaningful way to build a collection and enhance it. Although some of the specific models shown may not have served either during the time period or in the theatre, they are nevertheless broadly representative. These ships include Neptun *Sumner* (9.3cm), Neptun *Buckley*, Neptun LCS-L, Neptun PC, Trident LSS; Neptun, Trident Alpha and unknown maker of PTs and two Neptun landing craft. These range from 9.3 to 0.9cm overall length. Converted LCI, PCs (as PGM) and 40mm-armed PTs played a large role in barge-busting, after the Japanese Navy stopped risking destroyer transports to supply troops and equipment to their island outposts. None of these models have yet been modified. Note the differences in detail between the Neptun and Trident landing craft gunboats, as well as the three PT boats.

taught me about modelmaking and working with tools, as did the summers I worked at a professional model shop in Chicago while at college, primarily working on HO scale and larger models. Later, teaching myself how to be a jeweller and a photographer added further to my skills, sharpened my eyes and made me more critical of my own work. I believe in the comparative approach, of appreciating models from different producers with different levels of skill, and so I keep many models in their stock condition.

Like many other ship modellers, I tend to have a number of projects ongoing at the same time. However, for difficult modifications, I often concentrate on just one model although, conversely, it often helps to be able to switch between different tasks, so that the glue or paint can be drying on one while work proceeds on something else. Much of modelmaking is producing serial components prior to assembly, so an organised work schedule and clear instructions, even with simplified drawings, helps reduce stress and frustration. In the end, there is simply nothing like the satisfaction of having completed a difficut enhancement or a scratch-built model, especially if it is accurate and unique.

2

PRODUCTION METHODS

There exists currently for small-scale ship modelling a fair number of publications (see bibliography for details), as well as Kevin Holmes aforementioned series of 'Waterline Guides'. Both the websites of 1250 Scale and SMSC (Society of Miniature Ship Collectors) have information on model ship producers, ship modelling and dealers.

Jacobs has discussed the materials, production methods and especially how current European casting is accomplished. Wood or wood and metal small-scale ship models predominated in the early 20th century, and a number of very good modellers still use these media. Now cast metal (spin, vacuum or gravity casting) models are the

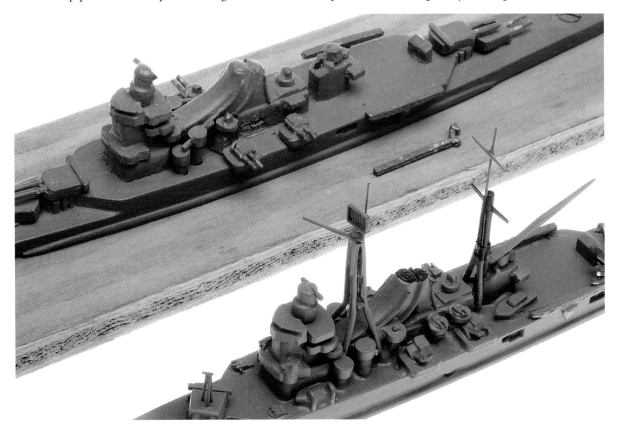

WWII recognition model of *Mogami* vs enhanced Superior *Mogami*: former on stained wood plinth, showing one of two screws holding it to base, and looking rather battered, without masts. Superior version has replaced 5in mounts with more accurate versions and added features like lifeboats and masts; further enhanced by author with

antenna masts on turrets, yards, radars, aircraft crane and cleanup of entire ship, as well as drilling out space between funnels. I do not know when Superior re-cast this Japanese heavy cruiser, but this does show wartime and post-war production, although both were probably still spin- or centrifugally cast.

most common, although some producers cast in resin. A few makers such as Triang and Framburg did die-casting, and there are still plastic injection-moulded models, perhaps the most expensive process, but one which permits mass production (as indeed does die-casting). Models produced by rapid prototyping (RP) machines are now used as masters for casting in metal, as well as production. While costs of 3D printing machines are decreasing, and many designers worldwide submit their computer files to output firms like Shapeways, quality at best may not quite match that of current European metal castings. Oversize features like gun barrels or other fragile items still appear due to the relatively weak strength of RP resins. The layer-by-layer process of 3D printing often leaves striations and the like, detracting from both detail and overall finish. Most current masters for metal casting are probably of hand-built styrene plastic or resin produced by RP, although in the past brass masters were probably more common, especially for spin casting or die-casting.

In terms of actual quantities produced, WWII recognition models comprise the largest number; in *Ship Models for the Military* Dorris states that major producer of military ID models Comet gave figures at the end of WWII of 3.5 million models made by them alone, comprised of 88 million parts, although these numbers include aircraft and armour models. Even greater numbers were later cited. Framburg manufactured most of their ship models by die-casting, which utilised injection of zinc alloys into metal moulds under pressure, although some larger hulls, like the battleship *Richelieu*, appear to have been spin cast with lead alloys. While I am not certain if all the wartime producers of naval recognition models cast hulls, superstructure, deck components and turrets separately, judging from those that I have examined many did so. These separate parts were either glued, soldered, crimped, swaged, peened or held on through friction. Examination of the undersides of models often reveal clues as to how they were produced and assembled. Comet produced two categories of models, the better

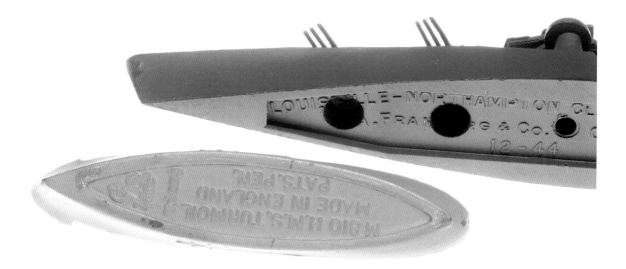

Underneath view of two die-cast ship models, Triang *Turmoil* tug and Framburg heavy cruiser *Louisville*. These models can be easily identified by their crisp lines and, in these cases, precise lettering, either raised or incised on underside. The metal is also much harder than most lead alloys used for small-scale model ships. Only the Japanese producer Konishi uses brass, on their lost-wax cast models, although I am not certain that all their ship and aircraft models are done by this method.

Bow view of Allied and Axis destroyers and escorts. These models represent some 75 years' worth of differences in production methods, from newest to oldest. *From left to right*: Neptun *Sumner* was an example of what had been state-of-the-art for European metal casting for decades; the Paper Lab 3D resin-printed *Winslow* destroyer is an early example of rapid prototyping, while the NN-CAD/Spider Navy metal HMS *Cavendish* is a 2014 purchase of a metal ship cast from a 3D printed master. The Montford *Davis* destroyer, mastered by John Youngerman, is a Resmet cast model, which has unfortunately bowed, as this resin/metal powder mix can be problematical. The Sea Vee *Loch Achanalt* was mastered, cast, assembled and painted by Sean Pritchard, who is British but resides in France. He is among the best producers in the world, using photo-etch and precise modelling; note no sign of mould partline, and the near scale thickness of the forward gun, along with very neat painting/decaling. Adjacent is an injection-moulded plastic Wiking 'Hunt', an extremely simple model. The die-cast Framburg *Rudderow* is a WWII or immediate post-war product, and among the most accurate of US recognition models; the AA guns were subsequently used by other

model manufacturers on their masters, an occasional but not unknown practice. Last is a wartime recognition Comet Japanese *Asashio*, quite worn, showing forward hole for screw to attach it to wooden plinth. To prevent lead disease from acids in the wood, such models should be detached from the base. Note that the quad 24in TTs are trained to port and starboard, an indication that such features, as well as the turrets, were separately cast and then assembled. These models range from 7.4 to 9.1cm overall length and are a mix of 1/1250 and 1/1200 scales, representing all the production methods except for hand-built; namely die-cast, plastic injection, resin casting, spin or centrifugal casting and one-piece mould metal casting/gravity casting. Using this method, some models may be essentially cast in one piece, but recent videos show others casting the hull, superstructure and parts like masts separately. Konishi of Japan cast by the lost-wax method. Certainly some producers make soldered masts, others may insert wires into the moulds to form guns or booms. Master builders like Peter Ohm of Germany show masters with cast guns of the type made by Neptun, so such armament may also be cast separately.

ones with separately-cast components and a second type in which fewer components were separate.

To avoid additional labour costs, as well as improving quality, metal models are now often

cast by European producers as one or a few pieces. However, recent photographs also show separate castings for the hull, superstructure and small parts like masts and funnels, meaning that separate castings may now be the prevalent practice.

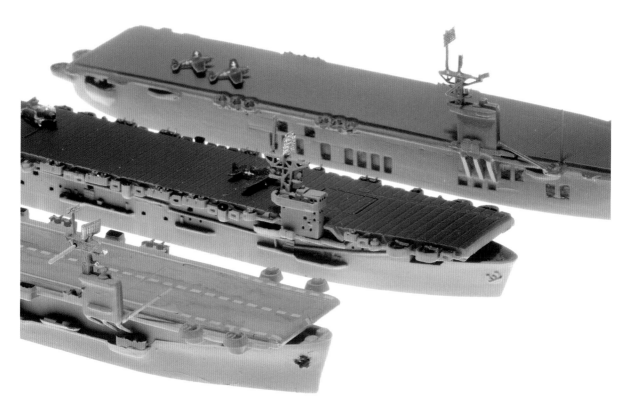

American escort carriers, *from top to bottom*: Superior metal *Sangamon*, Trident Alpha metal *Manila Bay*, Schlinghof/HDS plastic *Casablanca. Sangamon* has been detailed with soldered gun tubs, bridge radars, stern 5in guns replaced with guns converted from 1/700 40mm, with two Neptun Hellcats on deck, and is 14.2cm overall length. *Manila Bay* in 1944 is stock, with two Neptun Avengers, one with folded wings, and is 12.6cm overall length. Like the *Sangamon*, the deck and island may be separate castings. Plastic *Casablanca* is stock, with slight enhancement, and has Neptun Devastator on deck, not visible; the model is 12.4cm overall length and most likely injection moulded in several parts.

For example, Convoy Rescue Ship *Goodwin* (Chapter 21) had separately-cast life rafts.

Many WWII recognition models were more cleanly cast than their later reiterations, as features like the spaces between tripod legs and various nooks in the superstructure tend to fill in when poor moulds are made for one-piece castings. In order to lessen mould wear from undercuts, firms like Superior have cast guns on turrets with fins and/or flanges attached; these have to be carefully cut away and cleaned up. The latest Alnavco/Superior models may have done away with the above practices.

During the 1940s, centrifugal casting (also termed spin casting) was one of the primary casting process used by costume jewellery manu- facturers and makers of other small products, who spun cast white metal, primarily lead-tin alloys, often with antimony, into rubber moulds. In *Miniature Ship Models* Jacobs mentions that some European producers used metal moulds for centrifugal casting, but I have been unable to determine how such moulds were made or used. Organic rubbers, whether natural or synthetic, were unable to provide the long mould lives offered by silicone rubber, first developed as early as 1943 and subsequently introduced here in 1971; it possesses a much higher temperature resistance. For die-casting and organic rubber moulds for centrifugal casting, one had to have hard metal masters; it is a puzzle as to why there are almost no extant ship model masters from WWII. (In the history of Superior on the Alnavco website, it is stated that some masters were made of wood in the 1960s, which were sent to Taiwan to be turned into brass. Also listed there is who made specific models.). Die-casting required close tolerances for fabrication of the complex metal moulds, while for centrifugal casting organic rubber moulds had to be vulcanized, a process which used both heat and pressure to force the rubber to fit closely around the metal master, thus producing the cavity into which the molten metal would subsequently flow.

After the master was removed from the vulcanized rubber mould, gates, runners/sprues and air vents were cut into the two keyed halves of a mould, so that the molten metal would flow properly, without trapped air causing mould cavities not to be filled completely (see Chapter 20, where the metal did not fully fill the bridge deck portion of the mould of the Argonaut OBV *Cavina*). This stage of mould preparation is highly critical and regarded by some as an art; one can sometimes see evidence of such air vents in the form of traces of

Neptun IJN *Akitsushima* and Star kit of same vessel: the former is another great Father's Day gift from son Patrick. This seaplane tender, shown with factory-painted 'Emily', is often depicted in a very complicated camouflage scheme. The Star kit consists of hull and five separate parts, including the large stern crane. The turrets and mast/funnel are sprued. This metal alloy kit was possibly spin-cast and might make up to be a decent model, if enhanced. The models are 9.2 to 9.3cm overall length. Few producers currently supply kits like these, although current models may be still cast in parts.

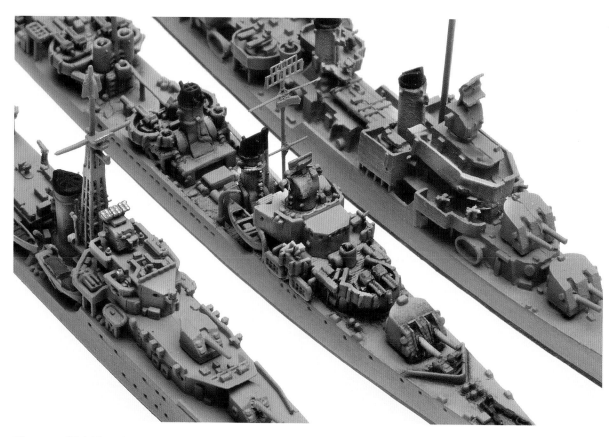

Close-up of British and American destroyers: *from left to right,* NN-CAD HMS *Cavendish* demonstrating model made with a 3D-printed resin master but cast in metal alloy; Paper Lab USS *Winslow,* a late-war destroyer; early 3D-printed resin ship model and metal alloy Neptun USS *Sumner,* using almost contemporary European casting, most likely from a handmade styrene plastic master. Note both cast models still show centreline mould part line but that *Cavendish* has finer detail, including the hollow lattice foremast, topped by a HF/DF antenna. Gun barrel thickness on all three models is comparable. The 3D-printed model shows the stepwise application of resin on some parts, especially the quad 40mm on the bridge superstructure. In the later Pacific war, even though the widely-used twin 5in guns with proximity fuzes were extremely effective AA, many US destroyers replaced 5in/38 turrets with 40mm weapons, these being regarded as an excellent close-in defence against attack by suicide aircraft.

small metal rods/wires/flash protruding from a model, which should have been trimmed off before painting. Many ship models show the centre part line of the moulds. In metal kits, one can see traces of the sprues attached to cast parts, through which the metal flowed into the mould cavities. Thin metal remnants of air vents are usually trimmed off by the producers before painting. Whether for centrifugal or vacuum casting, mould preparation most likely requires the same careful attention to metal and air flows if the casting is to be successful.

Recent online video postings by Optatus of Berlin show how this German producer casts, assembles via gluing, enhances and paints (airbrush and by hand) their models, beautifully demonstrated by the skilled and deft hands of Cindy Seelinger, who used to paint porcelain as a profession. Very few modelmakers have her extremely steady hands and superb hand/eye co-ordination.

Exactly how current European ship models are cast remains otherwise unpublished. In *Miniature Ship Models* Paul Jacobs states that during the 1960s there was a switch to single castings using thin latex rubber moulds. Ship model masters were dipped into liquid latex; when cured, the resulting thin layer covered the entire model. The latex covering was cut apart, the master removed (often being damaged during this stage) and the thin mould was enclosed with plaster, so as to be able to offer support for the metal pour, as well as probably acting as a heat sink so that the metal did not freeze too quickly. It is unclear if Jacobs meant latex or silicone rubber, but when using plastic or RP masters, both of which are fairly fragile, one has to use a mould material that sets without heat or pres-

sure and has great fidelity. A mould compound like the RTV silicones or similar rubbers used in the jewellery and dental industries offered these characteristics; most have to be de-bubbled with a vacuum pump. The lives of these silicon moulds are between ten and 200 castings, which can account for the very limited production of many models and is why one should look to buy models when they are first launched. Production can be increased by creating multiple moulds, but this can mean either the need for considerable repair of the masters after mould-making or else the use of multiple masters, both of which add to the expense.

Bow view of Paper Lab US destroyer *Winslow*, Sea Vee *Loch Achanalt* and Neptun German destroyer *Z25*: *Winslow* is an early generation 3D-printed resin model, with some photo-etched parts, representing late war AA armament where 'B' turret has been replaced by quad 40mm Bofors, to counter *kamikaze* attacks, while the *Loch Achanalt* is a very fine metal casting with a large proportion of photoetched parts of varying thicknesses. The Neptun *Z25*

was a mid-2000s purchase of what was then state-of-the-art European casting, complete with soldered tripod mast and cruciform yards, and well painted. All three models have been left as stock, and range from 7.7 to 10.1cm overall length. Note that in this photograph the models are essentially in focus from bow to stern, as this view was shot with studio strobes using a macro lens set to f32, which gives the image a very good depth of field.

Close-ups of *Z25* and *Loch Achanalt*. Upper image shows *Z25*, the level of detail, finish and painting, which can vary somewhat. Lower photograph of *Loch Achanalt* shows fine photo-etched structures, perhaps the most used in any small-scale ship model, resulting in a very realistic lattice mast. Note weathering and camouflage paint on *Loch Achanalt*.

Destroyer HMS *Cavendish* and Fleetline HMS *Amethyst*, 1944. Spider Navy/NN-CAD cast lattice mast of *Cavendish* very good compared to 1970s technology/modelling of *Amethyst* lattice mast, where the lattice is simply represented by incised lines.

A first-hand observation by collector and fine modeller of racing sailboats Rick Urudofsky on the casting of a *Langley* hull offers the most detailed information on the production process by Navis-Neptun: 'These are fairly hefty latex molds, possibly due to need for heat dissipation; they are about the size of a beer can to a one quart Coke bottle, looking like cookie dough. The mold is formed around the master under high vacuum, and then the mold is sliced longitudinally. The real art is inserting air holes with an approximately 18-gauge needle into the mold at critical positions, done by the principals. I imagine they must cast several sub-masters in the beginning, because the master is fairly ruined in the process. The models are cast by pouring a special metal alloy vertically into the mold, tapping it just so against a stone bench. There is an ingenious way to hold the halves together tightly, then quickly released apart. After casting, some models or parts need sanding to level the hulls.'

Close-up of late war DD359 *Winslow*, which is an early example of a resin model produced by rapid prototyping from Paper Lab, run by Darius Lipinski. It has a few photo-etched parts. While it is very detailed and compares well with Neptun, upon close examination one can see striations and other marks resulting from this technique, in which layers of liquid resin are laid down, then hardened by a catalyst such as UV light. The model still suffers from having gun barrels overscale, in order to reduce breakage when handled. Like balsa models, these resin models are extremely light.

NN-CAD/Spider Navy British destroyer *Cavendish* and Sea Vee *Loch Achanalt*: These two ship models represent perhaps the best of current (2020) 1/1250 ship model production. HMS *Cavendish* was a destroyer built in 1944 while *Loch Achanalt* was a Royal Navy 'Loch' class frigate loaned to the Canadian Navy late in WWII. Interestingly, the producers of both these models appear to be single individuals, Johann Ottmann for NN-CAD/Spider Navy and Sean Pritchard for Sea Vee, based respectively in Germany and France. The German producer uses 3D-printed masters for casting his metal models of a very high quality and precision. Without stripping a model and so dissolving any glued parts, it is not possible to know how many separate parts make up the *Cavendish*, but it is unlikely that this destroyer is cast in one piece, especially for the very detailed and apparently hollow lattice mast. By comparison, the Sea Vee lattice mast is of folded photo-etched construction and more accurate. By late in the war, many British escorts had changed from pole masts to lattice masts, in order to carry

more and heavier radar and electronics. *Cavendish* has a HF/DF antenna on the foremast, as well an X-shaped IFF antenna on the aft gun deck. A thin centreline mould part-line is still visible on the British destroyer but none is visible on the Sea Vee frigate. This latter model has a large number of photo-etched parts, very delicately etched. Since photo-etched parts are usually brass or stainless steel, they can be thin yet still have strength, not possible in lead-alloy castings. The 4in gun barrel appears to be of wire and thus scale-accurate, while AA is either cast or photo-etched. As well as the lattice mast, the bridge supports, the various yards, electronics and HF/DF antenna are all photo-etched. This means all photo-etched parts have had to be glued onto the model during assembly. The twin Squid anti-submarine mortars are very precisely modelled. Well painted and decaled, the frigate is both camouflaged and weathered. The downside of all these finely-made features is that one has to be very careful in handling models such as these to avoid damage.

Overhead view of US AA cruisers, both handmade and metal castings, *from left to right*: John Youngerman wood and wire *San Diego*, Barclay wood and wire *Tucson*, Neptun metal *Oakland*, MMM copy of Framburg metal *Oakland*, painted by W Croft, and Superior metal *Atlanta*, 13.2 to 13.8cm overall length. Note differences in fineness of hulls and thickness of gun barrels, from most scale-accurate in Youngerman to flanged 5in/38s in right-hand Superior model, which also has spines on aft gun turrets. The Barclay AA cruiser lacks 40mm and 20mm AA, which are indicated only by round discs of two different sizes. The other models all differ in their secondary AA, with MMM and Superior using Framburg twin 40mm though the MMM lacks 20mm. This extinct US Midwest firm cast models based on WWII recognition models; through mould shrinkage, these models are closer to 1/1250 than 1/1200. Best is the Neptun model, next is Youngerman. Neither model derived from Framburg or Superior have bow 20mm, only the gun-tub bases. Accurate US, British and Japanese 40mm, 25mm, 20mm AA and machine guns are now being produced by PaperLab in 1/1250 resin using 3D printing.

Recent observations by German collector and modeller Niels Neelsen about the Spider Navy HMS *Eagle* carrier made by Ottmann are informative and revealing: 'The hull is bare, the island is a separate piece, but all the antennas and the tripod mast are again separate pieces. Same holds for armament of the hull: all the directors and multiple Bofors mounts are attached separately, even the liferafts at the counter stern. So each model means a lot of handwork before completion.' It was noted, via a friend of Niels who did the computer-generated diagrams for 3D printing of a Russian cruiser master, that the master was composed of many separate pieces when it was moulded. Thus at least the better European producers now cast their models in separate pieces and then hand assemble. (They can also customise with paint, do detailing like steel wires for rigging, and supply protective cases for display.)

While few collectors know metallurgy, it is readily apparent from the hardness of a model's metal that many types of alloys are used for ship models, from almost pure lead to harder mixes, like lead/tin, zinc alloys and even some where aluminium might be alloyed with tin. Using the correct alloy is critical to success in casting, as the appropriate mix of metals determines the melting point, porosity, surface finish and strength. For example, pure lead (Pb) melts at 326° C, while tin (Sn) melts at 232°C; if there were a 60/40%

Pb/Sn mix, the temperature drops to 190°, most likely greatly prolonging mould life. Some producers make models with very smooth surfaces, for example those that are die-cast or some that are spin-cast, while others always have a very grainy finish, possibly from rapid cooling of the metal; this is evident especially when painted, even among the top producers. The anti-aircraft cruisers shown in Chapter 5 demonstrate some of these differences in metal smoothness and finishes, and also how paint reacts differently to absorbent wood and to metal surfaces.

***Maya*s after enhancements.** On Neptun *Maya*; work is limited to yards and replacement of broken 12.7cm barrels, which extend beyond the hull and are therefore at risk of being broken when the model is picked up. More extensive work carried out on Konishi *Maya*, with addition of copper and iron wire masts, copper RDF loop on bridge, Type 13 radar on rear of foremast, addition of seven 3D-printed PaperLab resin 25mm AA aft and on the roof of former no.4 turret, as well as considerable cleanup and adjustment of masts so that they fit properly. Foremost starboard 12.7cm barrels bent on Neptun *Maya* through careless handling. Both models are 16.3cm long. Neptun model made of soft Wismut alloy; that by Konishi has a zinc hull with brass superstructure cast using the lost-wax method.

3

TOOLS AND TECHNIQUES

Miniature ship model building is very much a solitary activity, heavily dependent on eyesight, hand-eye skills, patience, determination and the ability to translate complicated structures into simplified form which still remain recognisable as to their original function. I was first exposed to such small ship models when I returned in early 1946 to recently liberated Shanghai from the Chinese wartime capital of Chungking. In our *hutong* or alleyway, there were many German families and their children, one of whom had a large, flat wooden box full of German

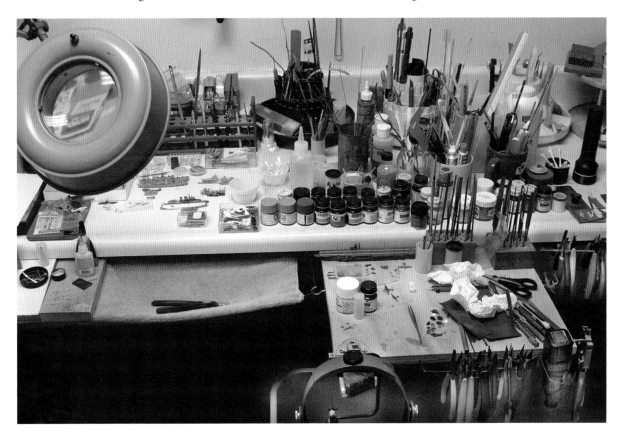

Modelmaking workbench, with various board extensions screwed on underneath to expand available working surfaces. Wire racks hold pliers/cutters, as well as slow speed Dremel rotary tool, hole punch and revolving hole puncher; screwed into nearest edge is rubber filing block, on which are hung Optivisor and jeweller's saw. On plywood board to right are drilled blocks with needles and larger files; to their right is another wire rack with pliers and nippers, while those I use most are in the rack visible up front. The orange fabric is a catch cloth intended to prevent loss of dropped small parts. Glues are to the left. Not shown is paper cutter, a very useful tool.

Techniques for building gun turrets, tubs and guns, *from left to right, top to bottom*: gun tubs, turret and 20mm shields made from aluminium quick-print plates, along with plastic; dapping block and punches for making round shielded AA gun turrets on Japanese carriers; making multiple British 4in AA mounts from aluminium-covered plastic sprue, with iron wire for guns, grooved brass rod for breeches, and rod for pivot; other AA turrets, partially sawn and with openings for gun barrels, finished turret and gun deck of aluminium and sprue; twin 5in Japanese mountings, including cleaned-up cast turret, turret with wire barrels and scratch-built turret; Figurehead 25mm AA improved by pinching out barrels with pliers; turrets made from aluminium sheet vs cast turret; newly produced PaperLab 3D-printed resin 1/1250 US 20, 40mm and Japanese single, twin and triple 25mm AA guns on sprues; German quad 20mm AA of wire/plastic strips and finished AA on *sperrbrecher Sauerland*.

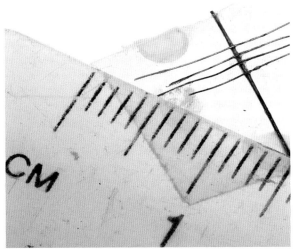

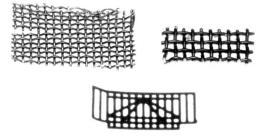

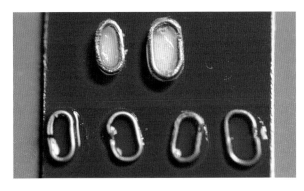

Techniques, tools and examples, *from left to right, top to bottom*: close-up of copper wires held onto wax paper for gluing, next to millimetre metric scale. After trimming, this will become a Type 13 radar for adjacent *Shokaku*. Fleetline and upside down Neptun Sunderlands, latter being converted to Mk V version, with underwing radar pods; it is easier to glue sprue onto wing for shaping, before trimming off. Photo-etched American radar by Navalis in stainless steel, with stainless steel and brass screens above, which can serve as radar aerials when trimmed neatly; smallest is 0.4cm wide. Close-up of finished Neptun Sunderland Mk V, with nose and tail twin 0.50 calibre machine guns, dorsal twin Hispano 20mm cannon, under-wing radar pods and dorsal radar antenna. Earlier Sunderlands were only armed with rifle-calibre machine guns, except for two single 0.50 calibre guns in the beams, and were no match for cannon-armed German fighters like the Ju 88. Oval wire rings glued onto plastic for making Carley floats; glue/paint will fill gaps in wire. Such oval rings can also be glued directly on a surface.

Close-up of enhanced German *sperrbrecher Sauerland,*
with all AA mounts crewed with Argos photo-etched crew;
glue and paint dabbed onto these flat figures to provide

depth. Single and quad 20mm AA and bow cannon have
crew painted in field grey, and a few additional crew are on
the bridge.

Close up of Superior *Shokaku* turrets, with and without
aluminium shields. The turret for twin 5in AA is composed
of three parts: a domed top, straight sided guntub, and
collar, not yet trimmed to size. Enclosed turrets are only on
starboard side, for those aft of the funnel, to protect gun
crews from toxic smoke.

Close-up of Hai *Pretoria Castle* stern. While I was
enhancing this British escort carrier, I noticed that the hull
was not steady but rocked when pressure was applied to the
stern. I then discovered that stern portion, now covered with
plastic sheet, was 1-2mm short of level. Thus plastic sheets
were glued on, sanded flat, then the gap between the hull
and plastic was filled with Bondo. When dry, it was sanded
smooth, resulting in a much more accurate stern.

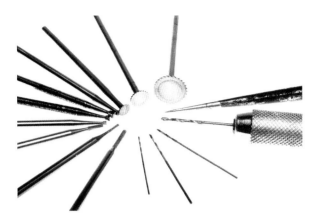

Burrs, drills and awl: an assortment of burrs, drills, pin vise with drill bit and sharp awl. Series of circular saws are crown burrs, in decreasing sizes; these are very useful for cutting off structures when modifying a model, or when a delicate cut has to be made. The other burrs are useful for hollowing out structures, for example gun tubs, and also come in a series of decreasing sizes. The cutter adjacent to the tapered burrs is good for cutting into metal, due to its straight and thin shape. Next to that is a burr with sintered diamonds, useful for delicate trimming. Drill bits of minute diameters are a must for miniature ship modelmaking. If you need to glue on a mast or something made from wire, the bond is much stronger if a hole of the appropriate diameter is drilled first. The awl is used to indent the material before drilling, thus preventing the drill from skidding.

Well-made tweezers are crucial for handling some parts, two here being Swiss Dumont Fils, one Indian modified with copper tips that have vertical slits to better hold small wires.

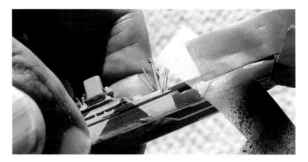

Use of Scotch or cello-tape as mask when restoring sprayed camouflage, as on this *Hokoku* model. If not pressed down too hard, this tape does not tear off paint when peeled off afterwards.

ship recognition models, probably Wiking. That experience, some seventy-four years ago, plus my late mechanical engineer brother John making and teaching me how to fabricate balsa wood ship models after we emigrated to America via USS *Marine Lynx* (T-AP 194) in late 1946, started a lifelong avocation, that has waxed and waned, mostly in relative isolation from other ship model collectors. When I am making jewellery, I am often not as careful as when I am working on a ship model. This could be because the small scale of a 1/1250 or 1/1200 model means that every defect shows up when one takes a close-up or detail photograph, which is magnified to several times the actual size.

While there are many talented builders of ship model masters, and rapid prototyping via 3D printing is increasing, in an economy where the decision to make a particular vessel into a model is usually dependent on its sales potential, there will always be numerous ships that will never be produced, due to a lack of wider market appeal. Thus scratch-building, conversion, enhancing and detailing skills will remain crucial to the collector who wants to expand beyond what is available on the commercial market. While I had kept a model work log since 1981, the need in the 2000s to document my time and work forced me to record in a much more detailed manner, as well as challenging me to upgrade and innovate my miniature naval shipbuilding techniques. Unlike starting a conversion on a well cast model, most of my work was often on substantially less well-made models; I believe that if I acquire or accept the job of working on a ship model, it is my responsibility to restore or improve it to a level I am comfortable

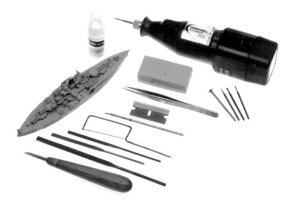

Tools and materials used in Thunderbolt project of Superior *West Virginia*: Dremel rotary tool, burrs, unfired polymer clay, forceps, safety razor, home-made brass punch, home-made saw, needle files, artist-made graver, New Glue and Superior WV.

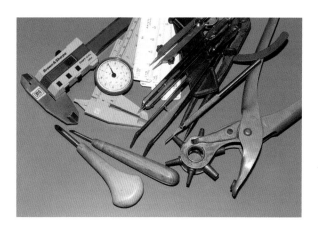

Hand tools and measuring instruments, *from left to right:* metal and plastic calipers, German Aristocrat multi-scale ruler (including 1/1250 scale; a gift from my late engineer brother John), three dividers, plastic-tipped forceps, miniature knife, rotary punch, and gravers made by New Zealand artist Steve Myhre, for carving soft metal, plastic and wood. Accurate measuring instruments are vital for small-scale ship modelling.

Glues: thick liquid plastic glue with needle applicator, craft glue (not too useful for small models), Zap-A-Gap cyano-acrylic glue popular among hobbyists although it does not have a very long shelf life and New Glue, thin cyano-acrylic glue used by beaders and jewellers. In foreground are applicators for cyano-acrylic glue (steel insect pins, plastic tags from clothing) and pointed paper strip for absorbing excess glue.

Rotary tools: Dremel rechargeable multispeed, Japanese battery-powered, Dremel 2-speed, Dremel corded (too high-speed and powerful for most modelling tasks) and Foredom jeweller's rotary tool, shown with chucks, burrs and cutoff wheel.

with. When working on rebuilds or modifications of models, it is crucially important to match the skill level of the original builder of the model, exceeding it only when the character of a model is not destroyed, or if the level of workmanship of the original model was terrible. While no one has commented on the ethics of restoration with small-scale 20th–21st century models, it is an issue with historical models. However, given the problem with lead disease/corrosion, distortion of Triang hulls and deterioration of the cellulose-acetate in recognition models, the use of multi-media materials and many different glues may create situations with long-term stability of current models, although it is unlikely that many will worry about this at the moment. Along with collecting actual models and improving them, it is vital to gather a parallel library of publications (both print and digital) and online information. Ship modelling cannot proceed successfully without accurate documentation; I try always to follow this practice.

That said, I am a firm believer that a model built with any level of skill is of interest, and teaches us about levels of ability or competence in crafting. In my vocation as a longtime researcher

Wider view of workbench area, with pegboard for tools, including Foredome rotary tool, lamps and the plastic cubes on both sides of my chair for holding models, additional tools and materials. Reference books and my three-ring ship modelling logs are on top. The kitchen counter top is almost completely covered with racks of tools and materials, as well as paint bottles used most frequently for touchups. I have screwed additional boards to the counter top to give me more working space, although usually the ship model or component is held in my hands for working. Note wire rack for hanging pliers/cutters, as well as two-speed Dremel rechargeable battery rotary tool, most used of my rotary devices; the 5,000rpm speed is most manageable for hand-held work.

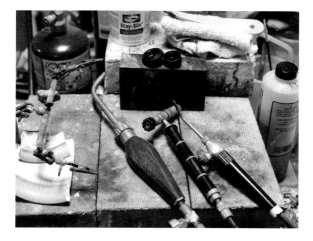

Torches are useful for ship model building, *from left to right*; acetylene/air torch, propane/air torch, with green propane tank in background and mini-oxyacetylene torch. Middle and microtorch are useful for silver soldering small armatures used on ship models and have changeable heads.

Array of useful tools for model shipbuilding: *from left to right*, thin flat nose pliers, needle nose tweezers, wire nipper, drill bit holders, hand-made engraving tool with wood handle, two-speed Dremel rotary tool, round nose pliers, Swiss calipers, Optivisor (absolutely vital for close-up work, with variable magnifying lenses), metric/imperial measure ruler, Zap-A-Gap cyano-acrylic glue. (I no longer use this glue as it has too short a shelf life before it hardens.) In front of Optivisor are some burrs, jeweller's saw (with removable thin blades of varying size teeth for fine sawing of all model-building materials). Within saw frame are glue appliers and absorbents, with red-handled sanding wand (these are colour coded for various grits). In foreground are craft knife with no.11 blade, dental chisel, needle files of varying sizes and varying teeth – all indispensable tools. This represents a selection of the tools on my work bench.

and writer about ancient, ethnographic and contemporary human adornments, I appreciate this aspect of human hand skills. In almost all fields of model collecting, there is intense debate about whether one should alter, repair or restore a model, and whether this decreases or increases its subsequent monetary value. That value to me is secondary to accuracy and completeness; used models are often devalued so much upon disposal that it becomes academic, although many believe modifications increase value, as do I, especially if well done. I prefer a completed model and most of my modifications would easily be detectable by an advanced collector, so there is no intent to deceive. The main impetus driving my own collecting and modelling came about through writing about naval ship models and the history behind the ships themselves, beginning in the late 1990s and carrying on to the present; one result being the additional care applied to my models since the early 2000s, as described in my earlier publications (see Bibliography).

Working on a model is essentially a multipart process: fabricating the hull, making the component parts and then assembling all these into the final model. Naval ship models usually have numerous structures that are the same, so serial production is required. This is often tedious and stressful; after several delicate parts are made, one has to separate them, which can result in loss or damage to a small part due to the kinetic force of the separation. Sometimes the knife or saw cut is not quite accurate, then requiring the tiny part to be corrected. During assembly, one has to glue these same small parts onto the hull or superstructure, often onto a thin wire. Most modellers use cyano-acrylic glue, which wicks onto surfaces easily and also has strong surface tension, both of which can hamper accurate placement of the part

Paint spray cans, bottled paint and modelling materials: Tamiya, Model Master, automotive primers, Floquil and GHQ paints, along with white putty, paintbrush, thin wires, plastic tags and sprue, odds and ends that are useful for ship modellers, as well as labelled paint samples on stiff boards.

More Tamiya and Model Master spray cans, with labelled paint samples, since spray paint colours rarely match those of the can tops. Automotive primers can supply a wide range of greys, but need to have samples/labels so the correct colour is used. They are also much cheaper than hobby paints. I use both enamel and water-based paints.

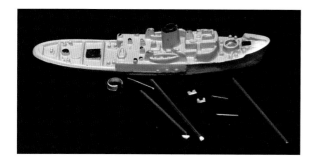

Triang HMS *Turmoil*, die-cast salvage or deep-sea rescue tug, launched 1944; details into a pleasing model. Arrayed are steel/brass wires for masts, derricks, yards, aluminium shields/bandstand and plastic parts for the mast. Bow bandstand has been burred to both deepen depression and thin the cast wall. 5.11cm overall length.

Finished Triang *Turmoil* vs stock Neptun US ATF, 5.0cm overall length, a very well-modelled deep-sea tug. *Turmoil*, previously without armament, now has bridge 20mms, aft 2pdr and bow 12pdr with three-sided aluminium shield. The paint was left as original except for some touching up, with some detailing lacking.

to be glued and the release of the glued part from a pair of tweezers. Even the smallest tremor of the hand can wreck such a procedure, so I try not to do such tasks in the mornings when I have had coffee. Evenings are better for tasks that require steadiness and concentration. I find that being slightly tired after a day at the office can often help model work.

I am fortunate to have both a model-building bench and a jewellery bench in my separate home studio, as well as a professional photography studio at *Ornament* (the journal we have published for 46 years). Having access to computer software for both photography and publishing as well makes it easier to gather documentation and convert it into print form if necessary.

Close-up of Superior *Kongo*, showing aft turret with brass cylinder around cast pivot, so that turret now turns smoothly, as well as soldered/glued copper wire antenna tower, peculiar to Japanese battleships and cruisers. This model has been enhanced and detailed, as evident from the mainmast and turret.

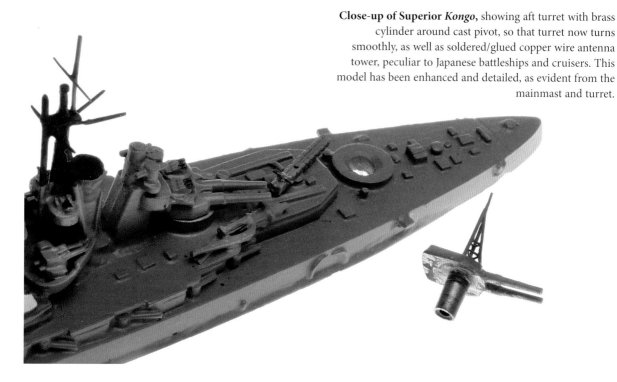

4

CAM SHIPS

Seaborne shipping was the vital lifeline of the British Empire. Early in WWII British convoys were threatened by German aircraft, such as the multi-engine FW 200 Condor, when they were beyond the range of land-based RAF aircraft, as well as by surface raiders and submarines. Thus thirty-five merchant ships were modified, equipped with catapults and service-worn Hurricanes to become Catapult Aircraft Merchant ships (CAM ships). The RAF supplied the pilots but the Royal Navy crewed and commanded the ships. The RN then proposed the Fighter Catapult Ship (FCS), which carried the Fulmar, a naval fighter – see scratch-built HMS *Springbank*, in Chapter 22. (These ships were later supplemented by Merchant Aircraft Carriers, or MAC ships, converted from oilers and grain carriers.) When launched by a rocket-propelled sled, the fighter could then attack or drive away the German aircraft. The pilot then had to try to land if an airfield was within reach, but usually had to bail out over the convoy and be rescued by one of the merchant ships or escorts – a perilous process.

I carried out a simple yet delicate conversion with one of Len Jordan's excellent resin-cast CAM ship kits. These 1/1200 models only needed slight work on the masts/booms, and for the metal Hurricane to be glued on, if one chose to retain the centre-mounted catapult. However, most period photographs show the catapult canted to port, so that the rocket blast would not damage the bridge or any deck cargo. I chose this latter configuration, as shown here. Since resin is brittle, I had to carefully cut away the cast on the catapult, enhance it, build a support tower, and file and refine the aircraft. Other small enhancements included

Warrior *Empire Day* CAM ship model, showing plan view of painted and enhanced model, with catapult canted to port side. Unlike FCS ships, which sometimes carried more than one aircraft, CAM ships only had one chance to destroy or drive away enemy aircraft. But CAM ships were fully functional as cargo carriers (as were, later, MAC ships) since in the crucial early days of WWII, every ship's cargo was vital; this model carries a deckload of Bedford trucks.

However, with having a bow mounted catapult, no AA guns were sited forward, unlike most FCS ships, which had a catapult mounted amidships.

additional antenna and a crow's nest. The camouflaged aircraft, raised catapult and painted Bedford trucks on deck added much to the attraction of this enhanced and corrected CAM ship, an important protector of early British convoys from enemy aircraft.

Warrior *Empire Day* CAM ships, showing painted and enhanced model, with catapult removed, vs. unpainted resin kit with centreline-mounted catapult, and kit parts. At least some CAM ships retained the centre-mounted catapult, such as *Empire Lawrence*, if there was not threat of blast damage to the bridge from the rocket sled. On the bow is a boom for paravanes. Note soldered copper wire catapult tower, and work platforms added to the end of the catapult.

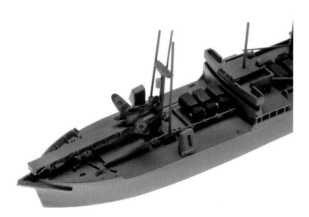

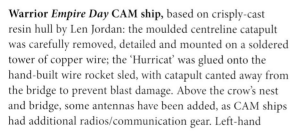

Warrior *Empire Day* CAM ship, based on crisply-cast resin hull by Len Jordan: the moulded centreline catapult was carefully removed, detailed and mounted on a soldered tower of copper wire; the 'Hurricat' was glued onto the hand-built wire rocket sled, with catapult canted away from the bridge to prevent blast damage. Above the crow's nest and bridge, some antennas have been added, as CAM ships had additional radios/communication gear. Left-hand image shows the catapult, before it was cut off and moved to port. Argonaut's well-cast metal model also has the catapult canted to port, instead of on the centreline. In combat, nine German aircraft were shot down (four FW 200 Condors, four He 111s, one Ju 88) and three chased away, which fulfilled the defensive function of the 'Hurricats'. Most 'Hurricat' pilots had to ditch, although one was able to land at a Russian airbase.

5

AA SHIPS, ALLIED AND AXIS

Virtually every naval ship or merchant ship serving during WWII was defensively armed to some degree, but because of the great threat from aircraft, many ships were dedicated to providing anti-aircraft protection, being either purpose-built or converted into auxiliary AA

There was a great variety of vessels built or converted in order to combat aircraft, ranging from submarines designed to fight it out on the surface, to ships providing inshore protection or for harbours, and those protecting convoys or carrier groups. *From top to bottom, left to right*: Neptun cruiser *Maya*, stock, 19cm length overall; Superior anti-aircraft cruiser *Isuzu*, rebuilt; Neptun *Akitsuki* destroyer, enhanced; Superior CLAA *Atlanta*, guns cleaned up, Youngerman anti-aircraft cruiser *Colombo*; *Prince Robert*, scratch-built by the author on 1/1200 balsa hull from the late 1940s – early 1950s, when the author first started making model ships. It is now 1/1250, reinforced at the bow with aluminium sheet as per the method of Frank Mantle. Completed 2013 but not camouflaged until May 2014. Repaired May 2014, after being dropped. Comet destroyer *Vanoc* modified as AA escort; HF *Medusa*, German floating AA battery, stock; usually anchored in harbours to attack Allied bomber streams; some had no engines and had to be towed; Neptun *VII C*, submarine trap with augmented AA; Santa Rosa *Aristocrat*, a paddle wheeler converted into an inshore AA ship, enhanced resin model and Trident Landing Ship Flak (LCF), to protect amphibious landings, stock, 4.6cm length overall.

Merchant vessels converted to AA ships: *left,* Optatus *Prince Robert, Ulster Queen* and Argonaut *Tynwald,* all armed with the same twin 4in guns, as well as pom-poms, 20mm and 0.50 calibre quad MGs. *Ulster Queen* and *Tynwald* have very similar builds, both with gundecks with zarebas for their main guns. Argonaut/Optatus, like Hai, are builders who solder their masts and other structures. While this is strong, it makes them difficult to repair.

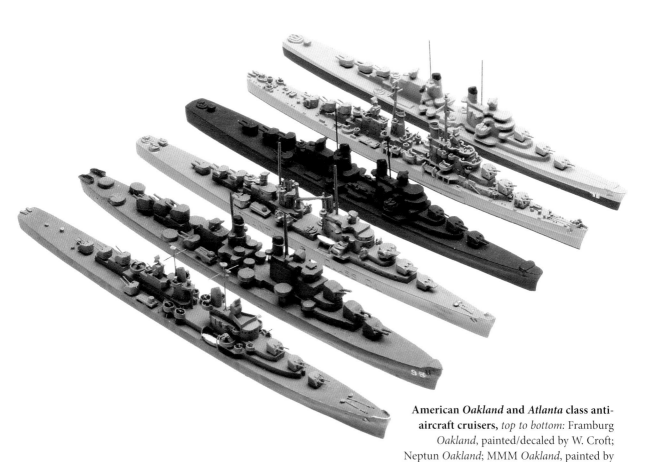

American *Oakland* and *Atlanta* class anti-aircraft cruisers, *top to bottom:* Framburg *Oakland,* painted/decaled by W. Croft; Neptun *Oakland;* MMM *Oakland,* painted by W Croft; Superior *Atlanta;* Barclay wood *Tucson* with round circles representing the secondary 40mm and 20mm AA; Youngerman wood *San Diego.* Models are 13.2 to 13.7cm. No other warships of their size in WWII carried as much AA armament as these cruisers.

Allied, Axis and neutral anti-aircraft cruisers: *left, top to bottom,* Hansa *Mendez Nunez,* eight 4in, no secondary AA visible, 11.2cm length overall; Neptun *Isuzu,* three twin 127mm, eleven triple 25mm, five 25mm, 13.3cm length overall; Argonaut *Jacob van Heemskerck* repaired, late war, five twin 102mm, four twin 40mm, two single 20mm, 10.4cm length overall; Neptun *Cairo,* four twin 4in, one quad pom-pom, two quad 50 cal MGs, 10.9cm length overall; Neptun *Dido,* five twin 5.25in, two quad pom-pom, four twin 20mm, five single 20mm, 12.8cm length overall; Neptun *Oakland,* six twin 5in, seven twin 40mm, twelve 20mm, 13.2cm length overall.

ships. Almost all Arctic convoys to Russia, or those in the Mediterranean, required a number of AA ships, similar to the American practice with carrier groups in the Pacific war. Early in the war, submarines, especially German ones, were perhaps the greatest threat to convoys, although as WWII progressed, and the lethality of aircraft increased due to more speed, armour, armament and payload, naval ships tried to counter the threat by up-arming, and this involved a number of considerations. Royal Navy ships were often so tightly designed that it was difficult to increase their AA capability appreciably, while US ships had more leeway as to space and stability. Often, it was necessary to land some other armament to allow more AA; this could be a bank of torpedoes, a gun turret or other less effective weapons. For example, with British ships, quad 0.50 calibre machine-guns were replaced by single 20mm guns

when they became available. The American Navy determined that it required twice as many 0.50 calibre rounds to down an aircraft as 20mm shells, but by the late Pacific war the Bofors 40mm was the preferred AA gun.

Both purpose-built and converted AA ships were not always stellar performers in their designated role. For example, from 1944 to 1945, CLAA95 *Oakland* shot down probably eight aircraft and assisted in downing seven, while CLAA53 *San Diego* downed nine. Other warships, like destroyers, even if not as well armed, often carried the brunt of anti-aircraft duties; for example, the destroyer *Callaghan* downed twelve kamikazes, and *Hugh W. Hadley* twenty-three aircraft while on radar picket duty at Okinawa. Of course, radar picket destroyers were among the ships most targeted by *kamikazes*. The most effective in downing aircraft were large US ships like

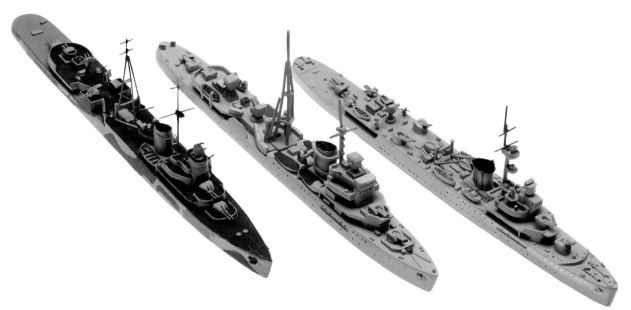

Netherlands cruiser *Jacob van Heemskerck*
by Youngerman, Trident and Argonaut, showing her in early and late war guises. Youngerman model was cleaned up/touched up, four single 20mm with shields replaced by six Hispano-Suiza 20mm in Plex turrets by author. Also balsa, it was camouflaged by Youngerman. The Trident

model (middle) is very inaccurate, with only four instead of five twin 4in mounts; while the Argonaut – in late war rig – had broken guns repaired and foremast enhanced. Size range from 10.5 to 11cm length. This view shows well the overall configuration of these three models.

British 'C' class, 'D' class, *Dido* and modified *Dido* class anti-aircraft cruisers in 1/1250 and 1/1200 scales; Great Britain and the Commonwealth nations used the most anti-aircraft cruisers (twenty-four), due to their need to protect large merchant fleets. Americans had the next largest number, all twelve being purpose-built in two classes. The Dutch had one, Japanese had two designated AA cruisers, the Italians were building two (*Etna, Vesuvio*) but none completed and the Germans had none. *From left to right*: Youngerman *Columbo*, Neptun *Cairo* (sunk by submarine during Operation 'Pedestal'), Delphin *Delhi*, Neptun *Delhi* (she was the only British warship to mount US 5in/38 guns, except some Lend-Lease CVEs), Framburg *Scylla* from the ex-Pattee collection, stored for some 50 years; the 4.5in guns proved to be better AA weapons than her sisters' 5.25in weapons; Neptun *Scylla*, Wiking modified *Dido*, Argonaut *Black Prince* (repaired/ detailed by author), Neptun *Black Prince* and *Dido*. These range from 10.8 to 13.2cm length overall.

battleships and aircraft carriers which were steady platforms, heavily armed with AA guns and equipped with numerous directors for them. By 1945, an American battleship could have 165 AA barrels: ten 5in/38 twins, twenty 40mm quads, eight 20mm twins and forty-nine 20mm singles. The battleship *South Dakota* shot down between twenty-six and thirty-two Japanese aircraft at the battle of Santa Cruz while the carrier *Essex* downed thirty-three. This does not mean large warships were immune to damage, as US battleships were hit or crashed by *kamikazes* nineteen times from 1944 to 1945, as well as HMS *King George V*. Over 50% of all Japanese aircraft shot down during the Pacific war were downed during the last twelve months of the conflict.

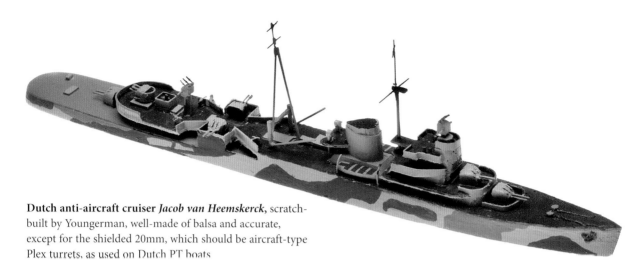

Dutch anti-aircraft cruiser *Jacob van Heemskerck,* scratch-built by Youngerman, well-made of balsa and accurate, except for the shielded 20mm, which should be aircraft-type Plex turrets, as used on Dutch PT boats

Close-up of Dutch anti-aircraft cruiser *Jacob van Heemskerck* **aft,** before cleanup. A Dremel-turned Plex turret is set alongside a shielded 20mm. When the ship escaped to the UK, she was armed with six single Hispano-Suiza 20mm in Plex turrets. Plans seldom correctly show these early war turrets on the ship.

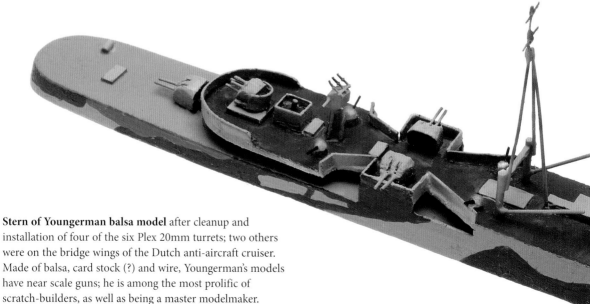

Stern of Youngerman balsa model after cleanup and installation of four of the six Plex 20mm turrets; two others were on the bridge wings of the Dutch anti-aircraft cruiser. Made of balsa, card stock (?) and wire, Youngerman's models have near scale guns; he is among the most prolific of scratch-builders, as well as being a master modelmaker.

Neptun vs Superior *Isuzu* anti-aircraft cruiser,
1/1250 and 1/1200; I traded for this bare metal cast;
inaccurate and made from a poor master, it probably reflects
information available during WW II; this may be a 1970s casting.
Superior model is 13.2cm length overall vs Neptun at 13.4cm.

Close-up of *Isuzu*, with cleaned-up turret, enhanced bridge,
along with radar, foremast, mast for direction-finding loop,
assorted deck furniture and bamboo to replace one of the
foremast legs. Bottom of opposite page is comparison of my
rebuild, with Neptun version. Instead of a lifeboat aft,
I added a *daihatsu*. Deck is painted to simulate linoleum,
used on Japanese warships. The rebuild is respectable, but
lacks the better-made weapons of the Neptun model.

Close-up of *Isuzu*, finished and painted, with white paint on
canvas dodgers at rear of bridge, deck not yet painted as
linoleum. If I were to carry out this enhancement again,
I would have replaced all the 25mm AA with scratch-built
ones, as the original cast AA are too poor, even with barrels
separated. Note single 25mm on bow, and yellow paint to
simulate the gold chrysanthemum crest, as on all major
Japanese warships.

Close-up of rebuilt *Isuzu* displaying details of the mainmast, made out of brass, steel, copper and plastic, including the starfish. The aft deck has been modified to the correct shape with plastic sheet and wire posts added. All guns on this Japanese AA cruiser were protected with angular gun tubs, here made of bent aluminium strips, using very thin-tip pliers. All triple 25mm AA guns had ready ammunition boxes situated nearby but the main-battery turrets must have had internal shell hoists. Both my and the Neptun model have single bow 25mm guns, but the actual ship would have had many more. When *Isuzu* was converted to an anti-aircraft cruiser in 1944, she supposedly mounted thirty-eight 25mm barrels; this model has nine triple 25mm, equalling twenty-seven barrels, plus one in the bow, leaving ten single 25mm unaccounted for. Wisniewski and Brezezinski in *The Japanese A.A. Cruiser Isuzu* cite no less than fifty 25mm, comprising eleven triple and seventeen single mounts. Photographs of a 1/350 scale plastic model of *Isuzu* show six single 25mm around her bridge and four more aft, by the stern 127mm mount. As with all Japanese warships, it is very difficult to know how many aircraft she shot down; I have only read of *Isuzu* shooting down an RAF Liberator in 1943, before the AA conversion. Instead of a lifeboat by the mainmast, I added a *daihatsu*, as these landing craft were so used, as seen in Wisniewski and Brzesinski's book.

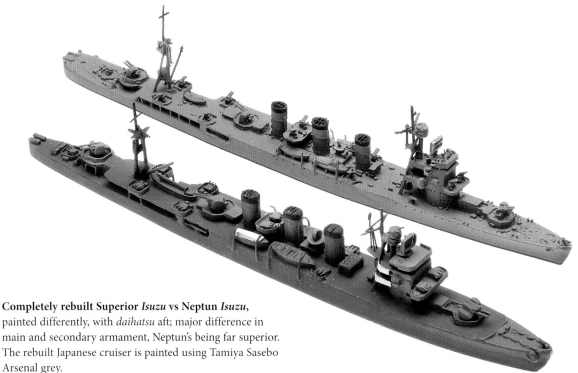

Completely rebuilt Superior *Isuzu* vs Neptun *Isuzu*, painted differently, with *daihatsu* aft; major difference in main and secondary armament, Neptun's being far superior. The rebuilt Japanese cruiser is painted using Tamiya Sasebo Arsenal grey.

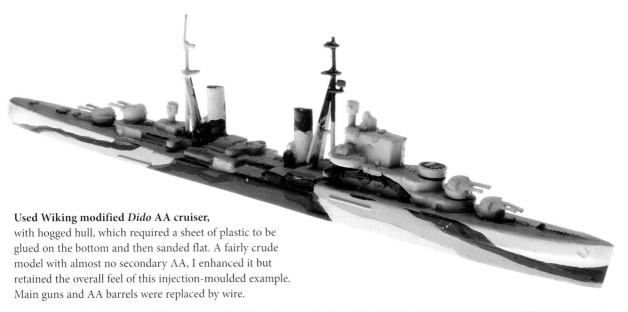

Used Wiking modified *Dido* AA cruiser,
with hogged hull, which required a sheet of plastic to be
glued on the bottom and then sanded flat. A fairly crude
model with almost no secondary AA, I enhanced it but
retained the overall feel of this injection-moulded example.
Main guns and AA barrels were replaced by wire.

Close-up comparison of modified *Dido*s, with plastic
Wiking model having had the hull drilled and burred, with
port quad pom-pom installed, made of copper wire with
aluminium shield and plastic guns and ammunition cans.

The damage and poor camouflage painting is apparent, as
well as the incorrect shape of the 5.25in turrets, not fixed, as
this would require a complete rebuild. Neptun *Dido* can be
seen behind.

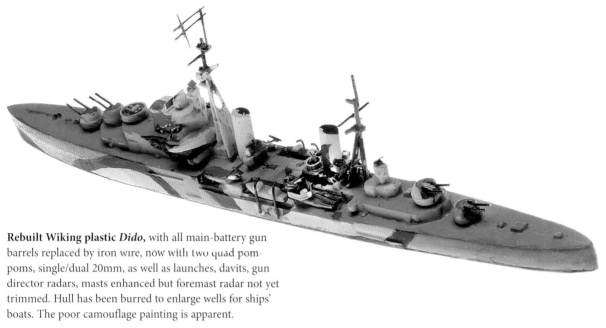

Rebuilt Wiking plastic *Dido*, with all main-battery gun
barrels replaced by iron wire, now with two quad pom-
poms, single/dual 20mm, as well as launches, davits, gun
director radars, masts enhanced but foremast radar not yet
trimmed. Hull has been burred to enlarge wells for ships'
boats. The poor camouflage painting is apparent.

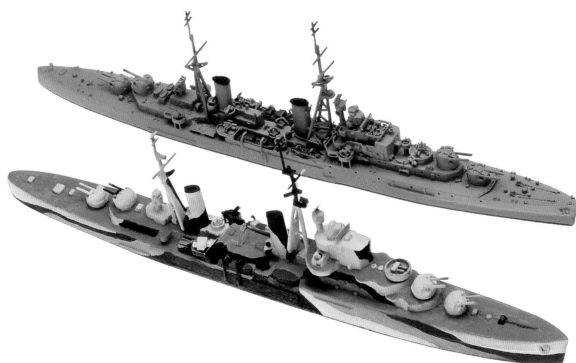

**The repainted *Dido* is compared with Neptun *Black
Prince*,** a modified *Dido*, 12.7cm length overall. One can see
there are still many differences, requiring further
enhancements to the German plastic model. Since this was
the only plastic Wiking anti-aircraft cruiser in my collection,
and its metal versions were used for recognition models

during WWII, it was worthwhile to put the effort into a
rebuild and repaint, even though it was made after the war.
My collecting theme is to have the same or similar ship
model from as many manufacturers as possible. The
moulded plastic *Dido* is 12.5cm length overall and was
probably produced in large numbers.

6

JERVIS BAY, HEROIC AMC

HMS *Jervis Bay* was an armed merchant cruiser (AMC) of 13,839 tons with a top speed of 15 knots, more than enough for convoy escort duty at 9 knots. It is ironic that this ship, which fought one of the most heroic battles of WWII with the 'pocket battleship' *Admiral Scheer* in 1940, is only represented by three models, all of which have flaws, although my image of the Santa Rosa model is of too poor resolution to permit detailed examination. Both the Colonia and Grzybowski 1/1250 models of this converted cargo liner have eight single 6in guns, no 3in AA and are painted in overall grey. They should have only seven low-angle guns, with one on the poop deck; two low/high angle AA guns aft; be painted in a medium or dark green hull, white superstructure, with buff funnel, ventilators, derricks/booms and masts; as well as a crucial low bulwark extending aft from the forecastle. (The Grzybowski model of the *Jervis Bay* as a passenger ship is, however, correctly painted in this livery.) The errors in the models probably reflect information available on the actual ship, in particular at the time when the models were made. If one looks at the many Internet sites about *Jervis Bay*, there are a few correct colour drawings of the ship when she was sunk, but most of the paintings and watercolours of her in action show the ship in overall grey (when converted to an AMC), varying in certain details, while the excellent 1/192 Imperial War Museum model of her as an AMC is also grey. All depictions of her in action that show her stern, as well as the IWM model, show *Jervis Bay* with seven guns, with one on the poop deck. A number of the images, whether photos or drawn/painted, also show the low bulwark extending aft from the

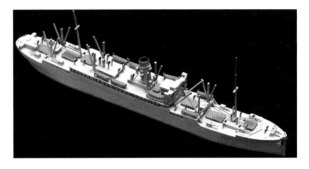

Colonia 16a *Jervis Bay* model, in light grey, with all plastic masts, derricks, booms and ventilators that varied greatly in size and completeness due to poor original modelling/casting. No work has been done yet. Duskin and Segman state she had gun director, rangefinder and fire-control equipment, but none of the extant models show such structures. 13.5cm overall length.

forecastle. While the book *Armed Merchant Cruisers 1878-1945* lists the incorrect eight-gun armament, a b/w photo dated 1940 and taken at Dakar, not long before she was sunk, does show her hull painted in a dark shade that would reflect the actual medium/dark green. *Jervis Bay* had been repainted in her original cargo liner livery to make her less conspicuous than in navy grey.

My Colonia model of *Jervis Bay* as an AMC was bought used and probably modified, costing slightly over $90 in 2015. Since I have had a long interest in such improvised warships, I very much wanted this model but had no idea how it related to the actual ship with regards to fidelity. I decided to undertake research to see what work was needed to make it accurate. The remodel/rebuild process began at the end of May and ended in mid-August 2017, requiring about forty-seven and a half hours spread over forty-one separate days. A photo of the Colonia model, from either the

Oliver's Welt or Sammelhafen websites, shows her in a lighter grey than my model, with all masts/derricks as wires and a few tall ventilators as bent wires, but the rest of the ventilators as cast, as with my model. As seen in my photos, there is no wire used on my model, while all masts and booms are plastic. The Grzybowski *Jervis Bay* AMC is in a darker grey, with masts/booms of wire, very cleanly and uniformly cast ventilators and boxy gun mounts. Neither of these models had breeches on their guns, a very definite characteristic of all AMC 6in guns, which had mounts open at the rear. *Jervis Bay* was armed with seven Mk VII 6in guns, but not the later boxy mount,used on most other AMCs. This type of gun dated from the 1890s, and of those on the *Jervis Bay* the oldest was from 1895. There is some confusion as to what type of gun mounts were on the ship. Duskin and Segman in *If the Gods are Good* state that maximum elevation of the ship's guns was 45 degrees, though they could only be loaded when at 0 degrees elevation. Older P.VII mounts could only elevate to 22 degrees, which gave the 6in gun a range of over 20,000 yards. If *Jervis Bay*'s guns could only elevate to 14 degrees, as stated by most sources, this low elevation would permit only a shorter range of 12,000 to 14,000 yards, outranged by 5.9in weapons used on most German auxiliary cruisers (HSKs or *Hilfskreuzer*)

which were often of same vintage but had more modern mounts. The guns of *Jervis Bay* were designated P1, S1 to P3, S3, with the poop deck gun designed as X. Initially, the guns had no shields, while those that were fitted to *Jervis Bay*, as seen in a very clear photo, barely offered protection to any of the gun crew, except for the two seated forward within the gun shield. The one available photo of a *Jervis Bay* gun crew in action shows about nine sailors (plus an officer), handling separate shells and bagged powder charges. The shells appear to be on trolleys, while the charges are piled behind the gun crew. The ammunition was hoisted up from adjoining holds. There are two large voice tubes projecting out of the deck, behind the gun, probably the only communication between the gun crew and those manning the range finder on the bridge.

I felt it was important to make the model's gun mounts accurate, as these were a defining feature of British AMCs, and so they needed to be hollow and show the gun breeches. Such features were probably not easy to achieve with cast mounts, so I had to develop a method of making hollow, sheet metal mounts bent to shape, as seen in the top image on the page opposite.

Duskin and Segman state that *Jervis Bay* had a gun director, rangefinder and fire-control equipment, which were all wrecked by the third salvo

Jervis Bay **after rebuild,** with five replacement sheet aluminium turrets, all guns fitted with breeches, two 3in AA aft of the lifeboats, with ready ammo box besides each. Missing davits replaced by copper wire, a rangefinder placed on the bridge, and crow's nest added to foremast. All ventilators have been built up with successive applications of Bondo. Bare metal areas have been sanded, filed and/or burred.

Stern of *Jervis Bay*, with two cast turrets removed and one sheet metal turret ('X' gun) placed on poop deck. Two cast turrets retained, with breeches added. There are two sizes of the final sheet aluminium turrets, as it appeared to me that the shields of the 4 forward turrets differed in their depths. Note the progressively reduced size of turrets, until final 2.1mm wide; one is cut/scribed, before folding. Red material is automotive Bondo filler.

from *Admiral Scheer*. None of the extant models show any features that suggest such equipment; I added a small rangefinder to the bridge of my model, which is seen on photos of some other British AMCs, like the *Alcantara*, *Carnarvon Castle* and *Laurentic*.

When *Admiral Scheer* caught up with Convoy HX84, Captain Fegen of *Jervis Bay* ordered the convoy to scatter to starboard, aided by a smoke screen, while he headed toward the 'pocket battleship' by turning to port, thus only P1, P2 (possibly P3) and the poop deck guns could engage. None of her shells hit the German ship, although one near miss was close enough to splash the enemy with seawater. The AMC was ablaze and out of action in 15 minutes but drew fire for two more hours, due to powder charges exploding on her stern, which made Captain Krancke of *Admiral Scheer* think she was still firing. In July 1940, 24,000 empty, sealed 45-gallon steel drums had been loaded into *Jervis Bay*'s holds and between decks;

it was this buoyancy that enabled her to stay afloat so long, despite being badly holed and effectively a wreck. (The crews of other AMCs also attributed a protective function to these steel barrels when a shell exploded among them.) This delay, and the approach of darkness, contributed to the Germans being able to sink only five of her thirty-seven convoy charges. Equally heroic was the Canadian ship SS *Beaverford*, which fought the *Admiral Scheer* for an additional five hours with her 3in and 4in guns, while making good use of a dense smokescreen from her funnel to mask herself. While London received the AMC's distress call, no ships were close enough to help. Later, the British sent two battleships, three battlecruisers, a carrier, five cruisers and fifteen destroyers to search unsuccessfully for the *Admiral Scheer*. Besides sinking Allied merchantmen, the other goal of the German raider was to disrupt the Royal Navy, and this she certainly accomplished.

While convoy rules dictated no ship should

Now correctly painted; green hull from spray can, a paint for use on blackboards. Somehow, the model did not appear correct to me when compared to photos and paintings of the actual ship.

Jervis Bay **with addition of bulwark** and starboard gun moved forward, being sanded smooth so no seams show. The gun mounting has been moved, as shown by the round dot and white paint aft of the turret. Note the difference in thickness of the gun shields on S1 and S2. The paintings of *Jervis Bay* seemed to suggest this, so I modelled the turrets accordingly, but am not sure if this is really correct.

turn back to help a convoy mate in distress, Captain Olander of the Swedish freighter *Stureholm* asked his crew to vote on going back to rescue survivors. Thus sixty-five of *Jervis Bay*'s crew of 265 were saved. (Sadly *Stureholm* was sunk by a German submarine on her next voyage.) The *Gloucester City*, sailing independently due to engine trouble, also ignored convoy strictures and rescued survivors from the tanker *San Demetrio*, the *Fresno City* and *Kenbane Head*, ships sunk or damaged from HX84.

This rebuild was among the longest of all ship model projects I have done to date, yet I feel good to have made this small monument to the memory of *Jervis Bay* and her truly brave captain and crew. A well-made and accurate ship model should be both a historical record and a tribute or memorial to the people who served on the ship herself and the actions they engaged in.

After an article I wrote about *Jervis Bay* was posted online, Paul Jacobs e-mailed me to say that he had a Colonia *Jervis Bay* with seven 6in guns, painted grey and a 1/1200 resin Santa Rosa *Jervis Bay* by John Staggs with correct armament, painted green, white and buff, with red waterline. In looking back at my photo archives, I discovered a photo I had pulled from the Internet years ago (probably from one of Kelvin Holmes' guides) of a Colonia *Jervis Bay* with six 6in guns and three AA guns aft as well as numerous other differences such as in derricks, orientation of the boom winches, deck furniture, a ventilator on the poop deck instead of a seventh 6in gun, a skylighted deck structure aft and unidentified features on the aft sides of the hull. It was painted grey, with black waterline and whitish decks, except for the forward and aft well-decks which were in grey. Jacobs thinks all these variations in the Colonia *Jervis Bay* represent different versions of the model, as corrected by the producers, who he believes started in the 1970s. His own model was purchased new in 1988.

Jervis Bay **after above correction** with 1/4800 CinC *Admiral Scheer*, for forced perspective. The take-home lesson is in studying all references carefully, and that in small-scale modelling, a few millimetres makes a big difference and has a large visual impact.

7

THUNDERBOLT, PACKING A PUNCH

The Elco quad 20mm Thunderbolt Mk 15 mount undoubtedly enabled PT boats to pack a bigger punch, especially in the later Pacific war, when targets for torpedoes diminished and landing craft or barge-busting became more of a priority, meaning PTs transitioned functionally from torpedo boats to gunboats. Additionally, it provided an early form of close-in weapon system (CIWS) against aircraft. Made by International Harvester, the mounts were essentially an almost square steel box, curved in the back, mounted on a tapered trunnion and turntable, thus capable of a 360-degree radius of fire, as well as about 90 degrees of elevation. There were a number of variations of the Thunderbolt, which were installed on PTs *556*, *557*, *558* and *559* in the Mediterranean, where German and Italian small craft such as torpedo boats and F-lighters were often their well-

Neptun 1/1250 + Superior 1/1200 models of BB48 *West Virginia* and PT Dockyard 1/600 and Neptun 1/1250 PT modified as *PT 559* or stock; Superior battleship, 1/600 PT and Neptun PT all extensively modified, equipped with Thunderbolt quad 20mm turrets. Stock Neptun PT is shown for comparison. The detailed Superior *West Virginia* is only partially painted, as I regard it as an incomplete project. Superior battleship has a detailed Neptun Kingfisher float-plane, Framburg catapult and running lights not yet painted.

The models range from 2.1cm to 15.9cm overall length.

armed adversaries. In the Southwest Pacific only *PT 174* was so fitted, which seems surprising, since PTs were so active in combating Japanese landing craft or barges there. However, according to a July 1945 report 'It seems it was the difficulty in shooting targets due to the rough ride of the Elco PTs that was a major contributing factor to these mounts not being further employed on Elco PTs.'

With the advent of Japanese *kamikaze* attacks, the mount was installed in 1945 on the battleships *Arkansas, Colorado, Maryland, Massachusetts* and *West Virginia* (as well as perhaps *Washington* and the gunnery training ship, ex-battleship, *Wyoming*) to serve as a CIWS. In fact, Thunderbolts were installed on at least some of the battleships, such as *West Virginia*, by July 1944, as shown by dated photographs. The weapon provided good ahead fire from a position on the conning tower of the older, rebuilt battleships, while presumably they were installed on similar positions on the two newer battleships, *Massachusetts* and *Washington*, although extant visual information is slight except for USS *Maryland*. According to Friedman's *Naval Anti-aircraft Guns and Gunnery*, the only criticism from *Maryland*'s skipper was that it was difficult to replace the ammo cans for the lower tier of guns. Only 60 rounds were in a ammo drum, so this meant frequent reloading, although there is no information about how many loaders were in a

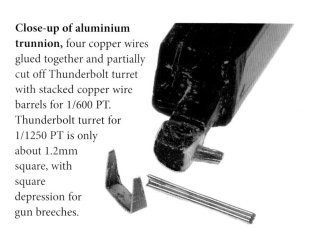

Close-up of aluminium trunnion, four copper wires glued together and partially cut off Thunderbolt turret with stacked copper wire barrels for 1/600 PT. Thunderbolt turret for 1/1250 PT is only about 1.2mm square, with square depression for gun breeches.

Thunderbolt gun crew, nor where ready-use ammo boxes were located. Only the gunner could fit inside the turret.

For the small-scale ship modeller, the problem is a paucity of available graphic and textual information on Thunderbolt mounts on battleships, with only one slightly out-of-focus photo of *Maryland* in *Naval Anti-aircraft Guns and Gunnery*, Alan Raven's plan drawing of the same ship in Friedman's *U.S. Battleships: An Illustrated Design History*, and a very grainy 1944 photo from the Internet of *Maryland* at the time of the battle of Leyte Gulf. The latter is a head-on shot, with the Thunderbolt installed but with slightly different gun-director equipment from that shown in the other image. Newly discovered archives at the Naval War College may contain more information, but this has not been possible to access at time of publication.

Having written about the Thunderbolt turret in my 2014 publication on naval anti-aircraft weapons (see Bibliography), I wanted to make an actual Thunderbolt model. I started in October 2016, but stopped in December, not restarting again until September of 2017 and then continuing on to February 2018. I had an old Superior *West Virginia*, partially disassembled, and a new Neptun *West Virginia*. I decided to restore and detail the old model and install a Thunderbolt on it, to show *West Virginia* as she appeared in 1944, to contrast with the Neptun model, which is in 1945 rig. However, the only logical placement of

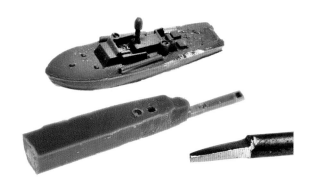

Partially stripped Neptun PT, with shaped sprue for Thunderbolt turret and brass rod filed square as a punch. Note test holes on sprue, round and punched square.

the Thunderbolt on *West Virginia*'s conning tower platform appeared to be partially blocked by the radar of the forward Mk 37 director. However, looking closely at the various drawings, photographs and large-scale models of *West Virginia* shows considerable variation in the amount of vertical space between the probable location of the Thunderbolt mount on the platform and the obstructing radar. So, there may have been just enough clearance for a quad 20mm field of fire, as it was a very small turret. In addition, I wanted to install the same quad 20mm turret on a Neptun PT, to show the mount on ships of very different sizes and functions.

To gain some experience on how to build the Thunderbolt turret, I started with a 1/600 PT Dockyard Elco 80ft resin model, which came with a Thunderbolt turret that had a moulded-on flat strip of four guns, and which needed to be considerably modified and detailed. The hull, torpedoes and gun armament all required work, in order to build a model that approximated *PT 559*. Other ship modellers have engaged in this practice, building a model in a larger scale, then scaling down to 1/1200 or 1/1250. For example John Youngerman has done this with 1/700 plastic ship

models, before scratch-building with wood or plastic in 1/1250 or 1/1200. However, working on the 1/600 Thunderbolt turned out to be frustrating and difficult, resulting in the approximately 3mm square mount becoming lost, necessitating building another turret and mount out of plastic sprue and aluminium sheet. This time, however, I was able to add four plastic cylinders to represent 20mm ammo cans, and install two banks of 28-gauge copper wire for the slightly staggered banks of 20mm cannon, the end result being a more accurate Thunderbolt. (Just as I was about to finish this, I found the original mount, in a previously forgotten area of my workbench; so the gods were either good or capricious. The newer turret was used.)

The 1/600 PT Dockyard resin model was adapted to the *PT 559* configuration, with a 20mm forward, sited to port, two twin 0.50 calibre machine-gun mounts, my scratch-built Thunderbolt in the stern, and four aircraft torpedoes on drop-off racks, rather than tubes. While this boat was portrayed in a photograph used for reference in Thayer blue, I just sprayed it with a slightly blue-grey automobile primer.

It is a considerable technical challenge to make

Stripped Neptun PT, with Thunderbolt quad 20mm turret; alongside are copper trunnion, turntable and an additional Thunderbolt turret, with two 20mm only. Turrets are about 1.2mm across.

1/600 PT, vs 1/1250 Neptun PT (2.1cm overall length), *left*, which has three torpedo tubes removed, as well as stern 20mm and other cast structures not on *PT 559*. Behind the Neptun PT is the partially finished scratch-built 1/1250 Thunderbolt turret, still attached to plastic sprue, and forged copper wire trunnion for the turret.

Stock Neptun PT, partially stripped PT and Thunderbolt turret attached to sprue, copper trunnion and finished 1/1250 Thunderbolt turret without base, on block of unfired Fimo polymer clay. PT is 2.1cm overall length.

such a tiny and complex weapon system while retaining its character in such a small scale. The Thunderbolt turret and its mount, as well as its quad gun barrels, is much smaller, more complex and fragile than anything I had previously built. As with many aspects of building small-scale models, one has to sometimes simplify and create an illusion of accuracy and detail, very difficult in 1/1200–1/1250.

To make the 1/1250 Thunderbolt turret, I shaped a piece of plastic sprue to the curved outline of the turret, then drilled a hole in the centre. A brazing rod of brass was then filed to a nearly square shape, and used as a handheld punch to change the round drilled hole into a square one, by pressing firmly into the drilled hole of the plastic sprue. Further lightly tapping the punch with a small hammer produced a better-formed hole. If a hole had not been not drilled first, the plastic sprue would have deformed too much. While not perfect, this offered a very reasonable solution of how to make a small, square hole. The trunnions were made from 28-gauge copper wire forged flat and

Close-up of stock and modified Neptun PT, stock with aft 20mm, twin 0.50 calibre machine guns and four canted torpedo tubes. This does not reflect late war PTs, which were much more heavily armed and usually discarded the tubes in favour of drop-off aircraft torpedoes to save weight. Late war US PTs carried more weapons for their size than any other warships. The modified model is equipped as *PT 559* in the Mediterranean, with 20mm forward, twin 0.50 calibre machine-guns, four torpedoes and a Thunderbolt aft, one of four so equipped in that theatre.

bent, while the 20mm barrels were represented by very thin copper wire stripped from a multi-strand electrical cord. Initially, I only fitted two wires, then decided that four looked more realistic.

So, within a space of a 1.2mm square piece of plastic, I had to glue on the above wire barrels, make a square hole, glue on a piece of plastic or aluminium sheet to represent the gunner's back-rest and dry fit a metal trunnion about 1.5mm wide. After the copper gun barrels were glued onto the face of the turret, it had to be clipped to size. The only way to work on such a small structure was to leave one side of the Thunderbolt mount attached to the sprue, while all the above operations were carried out, prior to the risky part of cutting off the turret, minus the trunnion, which had to be glued on after the turret was separated. Again, the danger and difficulty of working with such small and delicate pieces lies in how easily they are damaged by handling or how they can fall from your fingers or a pair of tweezers and be lost.

In order to avoid these problems, I took a block of unfired Fimo polymer clay and used the home-made punch to make a square depression and a slit in the clay, the latter as a space for the wire barrels. I then lowered the Thunderbolt turret into this depression, with the underside of the turret facing up. Using needlepoint tweezers, I carefully pushed the end of the U-shaped copper trunnion onto the plastic turret. The turret was then turned on its side, and each end of the trunnion was glued onto the turret with cyano-acrylic adhesive, by applying a minute amount of liquid glue with the point of an insect pin. Without such small glue applicators, it is easy to flood the work with too much glue and obscure details.

With one 1/1250 Thunderbolt turret completed and another needing just a trunnion to be glued on, I returned to adapting a Neptun PT to *PT 559* configuration, removing with files, burrs and Norton fine 400 grit sandpaper all stern features, the 20mm gun and four canted torpedo tubes. The alloy of this Neptun model was very hard, so it was difficult to remove cast-on features and return the deck to a flat surface without damage to the model. Besides gluing on the Thunderbolt mount, I had to add a scratch-built bow 20mm, two ready-use 20mm ammo boxes and four torpedoes, as well as replacing the mast/radar.

I then went back to working on the second Thunderbolt turret; after nine tries and about two hours of work over six separate days, I lost the turret. A third turret took 145 minutes over four days before reaching the stage when the trunnion was mounted. To make the turntables for the mounts, 28-gauge copper wire was melted into a ball, then forged flat, before thinning and shaping with 400 grit sandpaper into a suitable round disk. Unfortunately, after completing one turret, I realised the trunnion/turntable combination was too high, so these parts had to be removed, and shorter trunnions and thinner turntables made and re-glued. When completing the second turret, I was unable to glue on two additional 20mm wire barrels; it required finally gluing four wires together, which took an additional 70 minutes. All in all, this was an extremely frustrating undertaking, involving minute moves on which rested success or failure. The two completed Thunderbolt turrets were the most difficult model ship parts I have ever built, and yet even so did not really meet my expectations.

The old Superior *West Virginia* needed considerable work: some of the 5in/38 turrets were already removed, the remainder had to be either cut off with a crown saw or wrenched off with a pair of pliers as they had been epoxied on. After clean-up of glue remnants, damaged portions of the hull and superstructure had to be repaired and four large holes filled with round plastic sprue, so that smaller holes could be drilled to take the retaining rods/stems of the replacement turrets. Fortunately, I had some 75-year-old ones taken off a Framburg USS *Missouri*, which were die-cast and more accurate, plus the catapult from the same model, as well as a plastic crane of the correct configuration. Most of the 20mm guns were poorly cast, with portions of the gun posi-

PT Dockyard 1/600 model as *PT 559*, with Thunderbolt turret turned to port, 20mm forward, two twin 0.50 calibre machine guns, four aerial torpedoes and eleven photo-etched crew of brass and steel, made respectively by Gold Medal and Eduard. All figures are painted/repainted and heads/helmets made more three-dimensional with dabs of white glue. By the late war, US PTs had discarded torpedo tubes and used simple drop-off mounts. There is a gunner in the Thunderbolt turret. Note the smoke generator/exhausts on the stern of the PT.

tions filled in; these had to be burred out enough that the guns and shields were thinner and more recognisable as such, although still very poor representations. In the photographs of the Superior *West Virginia* before being painted, the bare metal areas show where burrs or files have ground off the metal and paint. The bow and stern 20mm guns/tubs were completely filed off and replaced by sheet aluminium tubs and fabricated guns, which matched the size of the cast 20mm guns, and were more accurate.

As with all conversions and reconstructions of model ships, it is important to retain the character of the original model. The Superior battleship is based on a wartime recognition model, with enough features to fulfil this function yet sturdy enough to withstand rough handling. Thus, rather than adding really accurate photo-etched radar, I chose to only mount one Navalis etched SK radar, and make sheet metal radars for all the others, which include the two main-battery gun director radars (Mk 8, Model 2), four Mk 37 radars and two SG or surface search radars. One of the primary differences between the 1944 and 1945

Starboard view of Superior *West Virginia*, showing all remaining Superior turrets removed and holes now filled by plastic sprue plugs, other burred areas and where Bondo was applied to fill badly-cast hull. Note the very rudimentary 20mm guns, much larger than those on the Neptun battleship, the quad 40mm from Framburg ship models and the lack of any radar. Compare with adjacent photo where the Framburg turrets have been re-installed and the model modified and enhanced, prior to painting.

West Virginia was replacing the 1944 SK bedspring radar with an SK-2 round, dished radar for 1945, as seen on the Neptun model. The Navalis SK radar has an elaborate back component, hard to bend and glue into place; it eventually fell off, so I only used the front photo-etched portion.

    An important part of the rebuild was to enlarge the platform on the conning tower; a thin strip of plastic was bent and glued onto the edge of the existing tower platform, then cleaned up. Then an aluminium strip was glued onto this, thus providing a bulwark. A thin bevelled plastic structure had to be fabricated and glued to the front of the conning tower; this position had portholes and may have functioned as a secondary bridge, but is missing on the Neptun model of *West Virginia*. I then dry-fitted the Thunderbolt mount; two 20mm ready-use ammo boxes were installed. The conning tower and aft gun director tower then had to be drilled to install yards. The soft lead alloy of the Superior model proved to be hard to drill, binding the thin drill bit repeatedly. Steel rods, for strength, were used for the yards and thin iron wire was fabricated for the rather fragile

Close-up of Superior *West Virginia* with aluminium sheet (turquoise-coloured quick-print plates), copper disks, steel and copper wire for radar and yards, Navalis SK photo-etched radar, masts of iron wire, aluminium bulwarks and Bondo to fill depressions in hull and superstructure. Bare metal represents areas that were burred, filed and sanded. Note Framburg 5in turrets and quad 40mm used by Superior for their model. Funnel detailed with aluminium smokestacks. Thunderbolt installed on added bridge deck.

struts. The actual yards and their supports extend out quite widely, but I shortened mine to minimise breakage from handling. The thin wire struts were pre-glued as Vs, by placing two wires into a V-shape on a piece of wax paper, to which cyano-acrylic glue does not adhere strongly. When dry, the Vs were removed by a razor blade, then the excess glue removed by fine sandpaper and the smallest possible crown saw burr. When delicate items like wire are glued, it is better to clean up with fine sandpaper rather than fine files, as the sandpaper is gentler and causes less vibration and stress. The wire Vs were clipped to size and glued onto the thicker steel rod, using home-made copper-clad needlepoint tweezers. With ordinary stainless steel tweezers, the iron wires will adhere during the delicate gluing operation, since even stainless steel becomes magnetic with use. In order to hold wire better, slots are filed or sawn at right angles on the tweezers; this enables a much tighter, secure grip on wires or other round objects when working.

The Framburg 5in/38 turrets were glued on, as they would drop off too easily if not. The final step in the rebuilding of the Superior *West Virginia* was to file a groove in the rear cradle of the catapult, so that the V-shaped forward portion of the main float of the Kingfisher would fit better. The rear portion of the float and the tail remained suspended. The additional gallery of 20mm guns forward of the superstructure on the Neptun *West Virginia* was not added to my reconstruction of the Superior edition, as this would take too much work. I also deliberately did not complete the painting of the Superior *West Virginia* as I regard this as an incomplete project, hoping that in future additional information will confirm the placement of the Thunderbolt turret.

During installation of a platform and SG radar on the foremast of the Neptun *West Virginia*, a number of the 5in/38 gun barrels broke off, since it was difficult not to inadvertently grab the middle of the model, where these soft gun barrels protruded beyond the hull. The broken stubs then had to be ground off and a hole made in the turret so that the replacement barrels would adhere better to the turret when glued.

After the models of the *West Virginia* were finished but not yet repainted, I went back to the PT models. The Neptun model had four torpedoes installed, as well as two ready-use 20mm ammo boxes, a scratch-built 20mm forward, sited to port, and mast/radar glued on, as well as a smoke canister or generator at the stern. While the third Thunderbolt turret was being glued, it slipped off and was lost, necessitating scratch-building a fourth turret; fortunately, partially-shaped sprue was still available. Four very fine copper wires had to be glued for the quad 20mm guns and aluminium sheet shaped for the gunner's backrest and the trunnion. I already had an almost finished copper turntable. The hopefully final scratch-building of the PT Thunderbolt turret required seven days and 230 minutes (or almost four hours) of additional work. Because this turret was made slightly smaller, the mounting process was changed. The copper turntable was first glued on to the stern of the Neptun PT, then the aluminium trunnion onto this and lastly, the plastic turret was carefully fitted onto the trunnion and glued. The last item to be glued was the wire antenna.

The Neptun battleship had added parts painted with Neptun touchup paint (the one intended for British, American and Italian ships), while the

Superior battleship was spray painted in light grey overall (Model Master 1933, Camouflage Grey), then had some black camouflage of her Measure 32 scheme added to the hull, using Tamiya Flat Black water-based paint. Masking was done with tape, with the port side midships pattern mask cut out using a printed image as a template. The tape mask peeled off some paint on both sides of hull, requiring further touching-up. Model Master 1933 was sprayed into a small container that held a few drops of acetone to slightly thin the enamel paint so it would not dry too quickly during touching-up.

The PT boats were spray painted with a slightly bluish grey auto primer made by Rustoleum. This brand varies considerably in colour, as do others, so I always test spray on a light card as reference. Then I number the test spray and the top of the plastic cover of the spray can, so I know what each can's contents look like. All 0.50 calibre machine guns and 20mm guns were painted with Poly S Grimy Black, so as not to look too stark, although a darker black might be more realistic to simulate the actual gun colour. It appears that guns smaller than 37–40mm were not painted on US

naval vessels. The 1/600 scale PT had eleven 1/700 Eduard and Gold Medal photo-etched crew added. Crew wore combinations of dark blue, light blue or white, representing shades of dungarees, denim shirts or white t-shirts, and all had olive drab helmets. However, the crew do appear slightly too small, not helped by the flatness of photo-etched sheet, despite the added paint and glue.

After going over my workbook log, the total number of days expended on the Thunderbolt project was: 2016 – 11 days; 2017 – 64 days and 2018 – 36 days, for a total of 111 days or, more precisely, 107 hours, not including time spent in photography, writing and research. All the photographs were taken at f32 with Canon 6D or 7D, 60mm and 100mm macro lenses, sometimes with Kenko extension tubes to increase magnification, and with studio strobes. One disadvantage of close-up or macro photography is that every little fault in modelling or painting is bound to show up.

This was the most complicated and time-consuming modelling project I have undertaken; yet I remain slightly disappointed that the details of the smaller Thunderbolt turrets have been some-what obscured by the applied paint, as well as being unable to confirm the exact position of the mount.

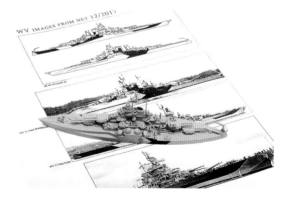

Enhanced/restored Superior *West Virginia*, 1/1200 and modified 1/1250 Neptun *PT 559*. Both quad 20mm Thunderbolt turrets are turned to port, barely visible even with close-up photography. Right-hand image shows Superior *West Virginia* in process of being painted with camouflage, all set on reference documents that I prepare for complex models – I gather all available images and information, and then print out on punched three-ring paper.

8

US AND JAPANESE
LANDING CRAFT

Given the large number of amphibious operations in the Pacific during WWII and the long distances involved, new types of ships had to be developed to meet these requirements. In this chapter I compare the American and Japanese responses to this need for transporting troops, vehicles and supplies from departure port to landing destination. Essentially both navies needed tank-landing ships and fast transports; the closest analogies are US LSTs and their variants, and APDs, versus Japanese No. 101/103 class landing ships and T1 Type fast transports. Of course, the US and its allies had far more types of transport vessels and landing craft

which were used for amphibious operations.

For the Japanese, the impetus was Guadalcanal, where they attempted to use destroyers, sometimes slightly modified, to transport troops for landings and reinforcement, often to isolated outposts. Due to the long distances involved many of these destroyers were sunk by Allied air attack while trying to fulfill these tasks. Thus came the need to develop craft better suited for landing men, vehicles and supplies, that were less expensive than destroyers, yet still had sufficient range and speed. But by the time Guadalcanal was lost, the Japanese were neither able to conduct many landings, nor able to

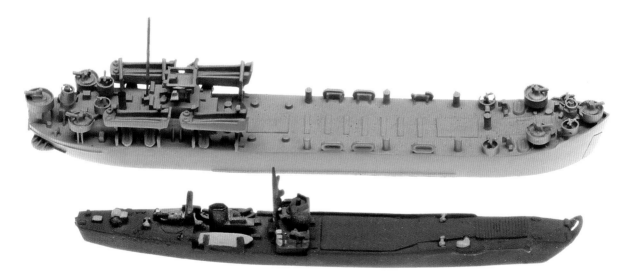

Neptun LST vs Trident T101 Japanese landing ship, illustrating differences. LST is of four-davit type, with one 40mm twin, five single 40mm and four 20mm, somewhat below the authorised AA armament. T101 shows one 8cm gun aft and two triple 25mm astride the bridge, although later they were fitted with at least nineteen 25mm AA. Maximum speed of LSTs was ca.11 knots, that of the T101 being 16 knots.

mobilise their industrial capacity to build many of such specialised landing craft and fast transports, which were given lower priority than other warships. There was also the need to simplify construction; this included electric welding, prefabricated sections and no sheer or camber to the hulls. Along with landing craft and fast transports, escort vessels like the *Kaibokan* and various

transports and oilers were subject to the same standardisation and simplified building methods. As the Pacific war progressed, submarines, including transport boats built and operated by both the Army and the Navy, sea trucks and landing barges became the primary means of transporting goods and men to Japan's far-flung territories, due to the toll taken by Allied

Neptun/ Sea Vee LSTS, middle is SV with LCT 5 or 6 on deck, lower is Sea Vee converted to launch L4 Piper Cubs, with pontoon sections hung off hull. All well modelled, stock, with accurate stern kedge anchors. Cockpits are painted on aircraft. These improvised carriers were used off Italy, France, the Philippines and later Okinawa and Iwo Jima.

Japanese landing craft. Trident T151, T101 and HBM T149 with very different hulls and as early versions. T151 does not have a stern kedge anchor, vital to back off beaches; it is 6.7cm overall length. The others have very rudimentary representations of stern anchors. Yorck versions may have slightly more details but appear to be rougher castings.

Neptun APD vs Trident fast transport, the former detailed with yard, radar, the latter has been cleaned up, carrying assorted Trident landing craft and a Figurehead *Koryu* midget sub. Normally, only *daihatsu* and *chuhatsu* were loaded, or a combination of subs/landing craft or amphibious tanks and *daihatsu*. Except for the 40mm AA on the APD, these vessels are fairly evenly armed.

submarines, surface warships, aircraft and mines.

The United States' answer to the need for fast transports came from converted WWI-era flush-deck destroyers (some thirty-six conversions) and the conversion of ninety-five destroyer escorts of the *Rudderow* class and the *Buckley* class to APDs. These carried four LCVPs, off-loaded via davits, while the Japanese T1 Type fast transport used

rails to unload four *daihatsu*, one *chuhatsu* or other combinations of landing craft, amphibious tanks or midget subs off an inclined stern. Initially armed with a 12.7cm gun and three triple 25mm AA, later versions carried seventeen additional 25mm and five 13mm AA, and were capable of 22 knots. The models shown here range from 1.04 to 8.0cm overall length.

Clydeside vs Neptun APDs, the Clydeside APD cleaned up, with crow's nest, yard and radar added. Even with two of the four boilers removed to make room for troops and cargo, converted flush-deck APDs could still make 22 knots. APDs converted from destroyer escorts had a top speed of 23 knots. *Rudderow* is armed with 5in/38 forward. Models are 7.4 to 7.8cm overall length.

Trident T1 Type Japanese fast transport, *Otten Eijo Maru* and Figurehead *Kaibokan* II escort, all modified and detailed, are late-war Japanese standardised ship designs with a simplified construction, but highly functional. *Eijo Maru* is resin, others are cast metal, sizes 7.75 to 5.5cm long. *Kaibokans* were late-war convoy escorts, built in an attempt to fill the gap in maritime protection.

Trident, HF and Figurehead landing craft/barges and Type D *Koryu* midget sub: rather chubby *daihatsu/chuhatsu* by HF, the *Koryu* is most likely a Figurehead. The four Trident Japanese landing craft are respectively 17m *Toku-Dai*, 15m *Moku-Dai,* 13m *Chuhatsu*, and 14m *Daihatsu*, the most commonly used.

9

SURCOUF AND I-400 SUBMARINES

Naval oddities are of obvious interest to model ship collectors. The giant French cruiser submarine *Surcouf* and the Japanese *I-400* class submarines were the largest submersibles in WWII, yet none of these vessels actually performed any useful role during the war. *Surcouf* was lost in a collision with a merchant ship in the Caribbean in 1942, while the two completed submarines of the *I-400* class never saw action. These latter were the world's largest submarines, at 5,223 tons, designed to carry three floatplanes with folding wings in their enormous hangers. Gun armament consisted of one 5.5in and ten 25mm AA. With a crude snorkel, they could cruise for 37,500 miles, the longest range for any WWII submarine. One of the *I-400* class was converted to a supply submarine while completing and could carry large amounts of fuel. Japanese submarines were often used to supply isolated island garrisons, and the Army even had supply submarines built to their specifications. My late fellow ship model collector and friend Alex White asked me to detail his *Surcouf* according to a model in the Musée de la Marine, Paris, which involved using some ordinary jeweller's techniques to fabricate a brass crane, including soldering, piercing with a jeweller's saw, as well as filing and doming the hanger door.

Argonaut French submarine *Surcouf* 1/1250 scale model, plan view, enhanced with long-range radio masts, hanger opened, detailed Cap Aero Besson MB411 floatplane with soldered and fabricated brass crane aft. Only 37mm AA guns are shown; machine guns are almost never fitted to small-scale naval models. Note rangefinder for 203mm/8in guns on the superstructure. The tall radio masts were common on French submarines, as well as trainable torpedo tubes.

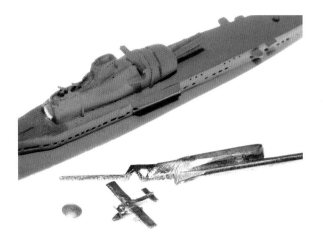

Argonaut *Surcouf* with two 203mm/8in guns, two 37mm, four 13.2mm AA, hanger for Cap Aero Besson MB411 floatplane; stock, 8.8cm overall length. France's largest cruiser submarine, at 3,250 tons surfaced, she was lost in collision with a freighter in 1942. (*Courtesy: the late Alexander White III*)

Details of conversion of *Surcouf*, showing hanger drilled out, painted white and domed hanger door of aluminium, cleaned up Cap Aero Besson MB411, with prop added. Above is brass crane being fabricated; it has been soldered and pierced with jeweller's saw. Below is the finished conversion, showing added conning tower mast, one of two radio masts, the opened hanger door, floatplane and crane aft of it. During the submarine's service life, the crane was shifted from the top of the hanger to aft.

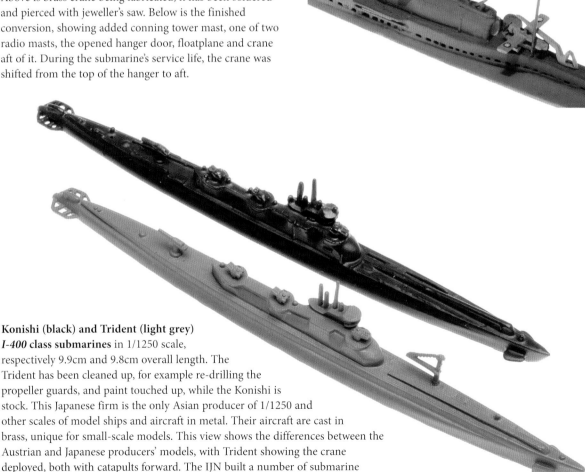

Konishi (black) and Trident (light grey) I-400 class submarines in 1/1250 scale, respectively 9.9cm and 9.8cm overall length. The Trident has been cleaned up, for example re-drilling the propeller guards, and paint touched up, while the Konishi is stock. This Japanese firm is the only Asian producer of 1/1250 and other scales of model ships and aircraft in metal. Their aircraft are cast in brass, unique for small-scale models. This view shows the differences between the Austrian and Japanese producers' models, with Trident showing the crane deployed, both with catapults forward. The IJN built a number of submarine classes carrying floatplanes in hangers integrated into their superstructures.

10

SUPERIOR DESTROYERS AND CRUISERS

Many American ship model collectors and modellers probably started their interest through some form of the numerous recognition models made for the armed forces during WWII. Huge numbers were made, in various scales, but the most numerous were 1/1200. Four firms produced in this scale: Bessarabis, Comet Metal Products, South Salem Studios and H.A. Framburg & Company. Products from Comet /Authenticast and Framburg were available for some time after WWII. Comet was the most prolific maker and Framburg was unique in that most of their ship models were die-cast, of zinc alloy and very accurate. In the 1960s, Ian Carter bought out the former Comet/Authenticast assests and began Superior Models, which in turn was bought out by Alnavco, which continues to produce Superior models. Both firms made changes to the models and moulds, so these are not truly like the original recognition models;

Enhanced Superior *Fletcher,* a mid-war round-bridge ship armed with five single 5in/38, one quad and two twin 40mm, nine 20mm, two quintuple TT, depth charge rack and throwers, as well as radars, electronic sensors, and a funnel spreader, unusual for US warships. In the late Pacific war, with the *kamikaze* threat, US destroyers discarded main guns or TTs in order to increase 40mm AA, as 20mm were not powerful enough to prevent Japanese aircraft from crashing into these ships, which were among the most badly hit in this way.

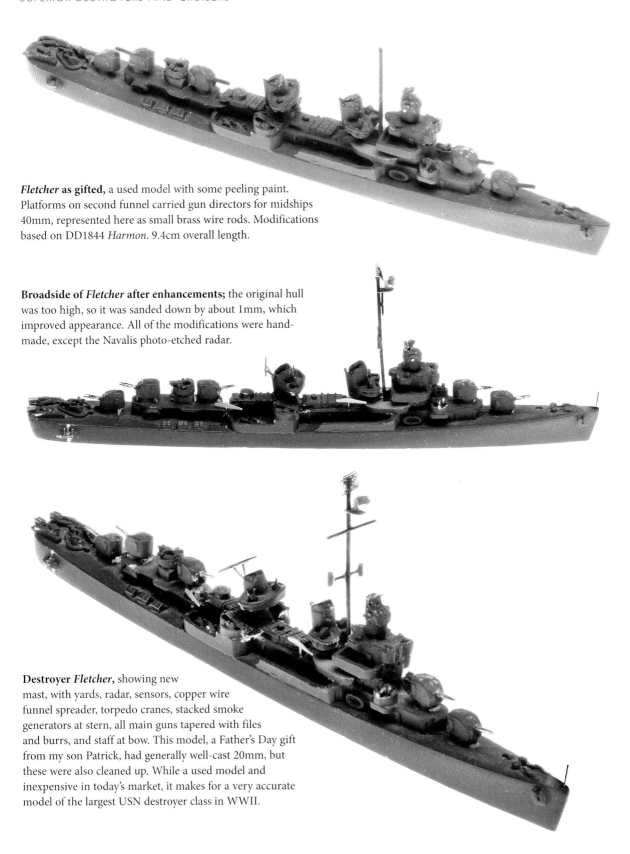

Fletcher **as gifted,** a used model with some peeling paint. Platforms on second funnel carried gun directors for midships 40mm, represented here as small brass wire rods. Modifications based on DD1844 *Harmon*. 9.4cm overall length.

Broadside of *Fletcher* **after enhancements;** the original hull was too high, so it was sanded down by about 1mm, which improved appearance. All of the modifications were hand-made, except the Navalis photo-etched radar.

Destroyer *Fletcher,* showing new mast, with yards, radar, sensors, copper wire funnel spreader, torpedo cranes, stacked smoke generators at stern, all main guns tapered with files and burrs, and staff at bow. This model, a Father's Day gift from my son Patrick, had generally well-cast 20mm, but these were also cleaned up. While a used model and inexpensive in today's market, it makes for a very accurate model of the largest USN destroyer class in WWII.

however authentic wartime recognition models are still available.

Many recognition models were cast as separate parts, hull and superstructure, with individual weapons and masts. Due to the large workforces of the 1940s, firms could afford to assemble these models. After the war, firms made their moulds from complete models, so that often areas between separate structures filled in, resulting in much poorer castings and models. Other alterations to moulds, such as fins projecting from gun barrels, were to extend mould life. Thus if one is to enhance or convert such ship models, earlier versions are usually more desirable. However, much of the satisfaction of altering models comes from how much one can actually improve on a poor model, so this does not matter much for those dedicated to making their collections more accurate. I have both authentic wartime recognition models, which often came screwed onto wooden plinths, as well as later versions produced after the war. Usually, I keep true recognition models intact, although detached from their bases as wood acids can deteriorate metal and are thought to be the cause of the dreaded lead disease or corrosion that has destroyed many lead alloy models. Recognition models in 1/500 scale made of injected cellulose acetate plastic are also subject to a dangerous condition resulting from excessive shrinking, resulting in the model breaking into pieces.

I received models made by Authenticast when family members visited Polk's Hobby in New York City, while I also bought Framburg models from the museum store of the Museum of Science and Industry when I lived in Chicago during my high school and college years.

In this and other chapters, I show how I enhanced various models having a heritage from recognition models. For those with a sense of history, it is easy to imagine how such models served Allied and Axis armed forces, although I am only aware of American, British, German and Japanese recognition models. Allied recognition models of interest to small ship collectors are in 1/1200 scale (although 1/300, 1/500, 1/600 and other very small scales, 1/2000–1/5000, were made), while German ones are in 1/1250, and were made by Wiking. I have written about rare

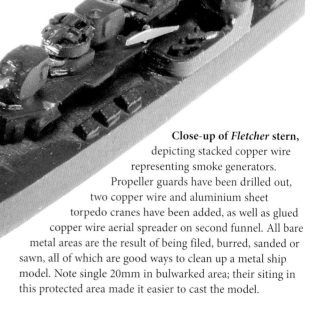

Close-up of *Fletcher* stern, depicting stacked copper wire representing smoke generators. Propeller guards have been drilled out, two copper wire and aluminium sheet torpedo cranes have been added, as well as glued copper wire aerial spreader on second funnel. All bare metal areas are the result of being filed, burred, sanded or sawn, all of which are good ways to clean up a metal ship model. Note single 20mm in bulwarked area; their siting in this protected area made it easier to cast the model.

Detail of Superior *Le Fantasque,* which had gun barrels cast with fins, as well as a little cleaning up required of casting residues. Fins protect the rubber mould from undercuts and prolongs life of moulds but make the model hard to fix. Light AA on bridge have filled in and are almost unrecognisable as such.

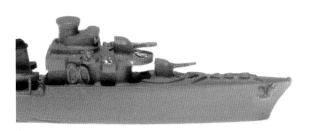

Same French destroyer after cleaning up, with gun barrels now exposed and thinned/tapered, and light AA burred out, before further conversion. Many French vessels received refits at US shipyards, so they were often equipped with American 20mm and 40mm AA guns.

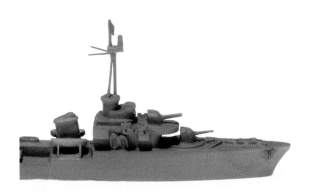

***Le Fantasque* nearing completion of enhancement,** with tripod mast, yards and American radar, as well as four 20mm AA on the bridge, now made of separate shields and gun barrels. While not as detailed as German models, it is certainly a presentable model and carries the legacy of its former role as a wartime recognition model. The model still awaits final paint detailing. (*Courtesy of the late Alexander White III*)

Japanese recognition models in 1/500 scale and there have been recent auction sales at Bonhams of Japanese recognition models ranging from $12,000 to $24,000, although the scale was not given. American recognition models sell for much less, unless they are rare and complete sets. Recent acquisitions of rare Japanese recognition models are shown in Chapter 1.

This chapter covers enhancements I have done on French and American warship models, but elsewhere I have done the same for other navies. Almost any technique applied to one type of model can be easily used for others, no matter the medium, although modifying or repairing zinc alloy models is the most difficult, due to the hardness of the metal and the difficulty of gluing. Many of the enhancements and modifications I

make are to bring out or restore characteristic features of the different navies, such as the cruciform yards of French and German ships, or the raked yards of Japanese vessels. American ships have easily-identifiable masts, usually arrayed with radars and sensors, like in the *Fletcher* class destroyer shown. The most satisfactory type of enhancement or modification is for someone who has personally served on a warship in WWII, or had a family member who did so, such as when I made models of ships that my late brother-in-law John Bainbridge commanded, or for a friend whose father served on various French destroyers and heavy cruisers. Her mother worked at the Philadelphia Navy Yard and met her French sailor husband when his ship was being refitted there during the war.

Enhanced Superior French destroyer *Le Hardi,* which has been cleaned up, with mast and cruciform yard installed, along with funnel antenna or aerial spreaders. This feature required soldering copper wires, as in foreground, which were bent into shape and glued. Both French and German destroyers of WWII used cruciform yards, the fabrication of which requires gluing of two V-shaped wires onto the mast. Boat cranes and light AA were added to base model before repainting.

Superior French heavy cruiser *Tourville,* possibly adapted from a *Suffren*, on which upper bridge support was cast as separate rods. Moderate detailing on background model; foreground ship has had filled-in areas pierced and sawn out, with one tripod leg replaced by brass rod. Mast, yard, crow's nest and light AA added.

11

JEAN BART, FRENCH BATTLESHIP

This series of conversions, of a Comet *Richelieu* into *Jean Bart* as in November 1942, began with a $3.50 1/1200 wartime ID model bought approximately 70 years ago by my late good friend and fellow model collector Alex White. He had begun the process of stripping this very soft, high lead alloy ship model, but had not finished in 2009, when he commissioned me to upgrade his large fleet of French naval ship models, consisting of over 200 ships and 41 aircraft. Working with photocopied reference material and whatever images and information were then available on the Internet, primarily very grainy reconnaissance photos taken by carrier aircraft from USS *Ranger*, I drew conversion plans and worked for some ten hours, across about 20 days, to finish the first conversion. My AA armament was still not accurate in number or type, as none of the numerous machine-guns were installed, nor all the 37mm guns. Paul Jacobs, an American with perhaps the largest ship model collection in the US, as well as a model producer (Saratoga Shipyard), made his *Jean Bart* conversion from a Neptun *Richelieu* much more detailed and complete. His conversion had at least five 90mm twin turrets and at least twenty-four single and dual 37mm and 13.2mm AA guns and machine guns. The entire process is detailed on his website, 1250scale.com and is entitled 'Yellow Battleship'.

His conversion was done entirely with plastic scratch-built parts, although mine was done primarily with metal sheet and wire, and included soldering the frame of the skeleton of turret II from forged/flattened copper wire. Five months after the *Richelieu/Jean Bart* conversion was finished, White acquired a copy of the book *French Battleships 1922-1956* by John Jordan and Robert Dumas, which provided excellent text and new illustrations, though unfortunately no plan views of *Jean Bart* in the autumn of 1942. So, like

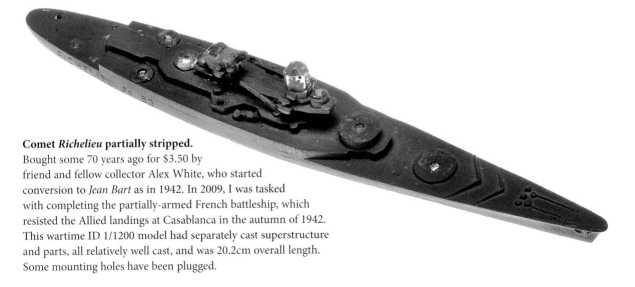

Comet *Richelieu* partially stripped.
Bought some 70 years ago for $3.50 by friend and fellow collector Alex White, who started conversion to *Jean Bart* as in 1942. In 2009, I was tasked with completing the partially-armed French battleship, which resisted the Allied landings at Casablanca in the autumn of 1942. This wartime ID 1/1200 model had separately cast superstructure and parts, all relatively well cast, and was 20.2cm overall length. Some mounting holes have been plugged.

Close-up of soldered and glued copper, aluminium and plastic skeleton of turret II, intended for four 380mm guns. A midline length-wise partition separated each pair of guns, as can be seen. Below the skeleton the turret is almost completed. Alongside is an anchor of brass and copper wire, soldered and forged or flattened. During the initial conversion, I did not have access to the excellent information and images provided in Jordan and Dumas' *French Battleships 1922-1956*, and therefore inaccuracies occurred.

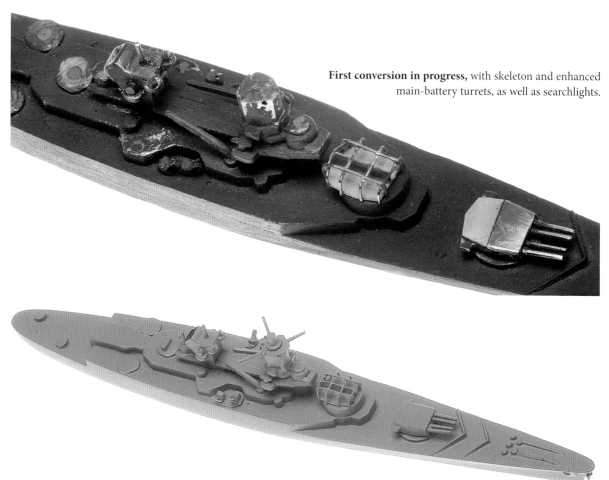

First conversion in progress, with skeleton and enhanced main-battery turrets, as well as searchlights.

Finished first conversion with bridge complete, assorted AA installed and ship painted in tan or adobe, to blend in with nearby dockside warehouses and grain silos. The AA armament is not accurate, being much fewer than the 90mm, 37mm, 13.2mm and 8mm cannons and machine guns listed by Jordan and Dumas in their book *French Battleships 1922-1956*, with only a few 90mm and 37mm weapons installed.

the actual ship, the model underwent another rebuild: this entailed siting DEM radars on the bridge, a gun director on the now partially armoured skeleton turret, two 90mm sub-calibre practice guns to each side of turret I and three additional 37mm AA. I did not mount the four 13.2mm dual machine guns on the bridge. Even with the drawings of French 37mm AA guns in Campbell's *Naval Weapons of World War II*, it was difficult to fabricate ones that showed the distinctive features of these guns. Additional lifeboats

were not fabricated and installed, so my conversion still did not match the actual *Jean Bart* at the time of the Allied invasion, Operation 'Torch'. She was badly damaged by 16in shellfire from USS *Massachusetts*, as well as bombs from Dauntless dive bombers flown off USS *Ranger*. Jordan and Dumas show exactly the damage done by the seven 16in shells. It was proposed that the battleship would be re-armed and completed in the US but, unlike her sister ship *Richelieu*, *Jean Bart* was never repaired/re-armed during WWII.

Five months after first conversion, Jordan and Dumas's book became available, providing more accurate colour and structural information. Main turret II was partially armoured at front and rear, and a small gun director was installed on the top armor; these features were added, as well as a 90mm sub-calibre gun on each side of turret I, while

bridge, mast and radars were painted black and additional 37mm AA fitted, as seen on the starboard side of the skeleton turret. The ship was again sprayed grey, to check fit and finish, before repainting in a new yellow. Aluminium sheet, copper and brass wire were used for additional armament and features.

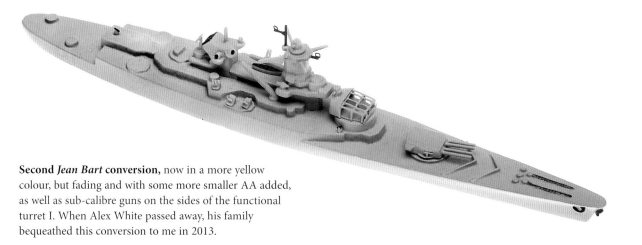

Second *Jean Bart* conversion, now in a more yellow colour, but fading and with some more smaller AA added, as well as sub-calibre guns on the sides of the functional turret I. When Alex White passed away, his family bequeathed this conversion to me in 2013.

12

AIRCRAFT CARRIERS

Aircraft carriers were considered the most important warships in WWII, especially in the Pacific, although surface combat still played a prominent role. Since I tend not to collect capital ships, I have only one large carrier, a used Superior *Shokaku* that has received moderate enhancement. Many in my model ship collection fall under the category of conversion for war. The US Navy and the Royal Navy (including the Commonwealth navies) employed a large variety of carriers but among the Axis powers, only the Japanese had operational aircraft carriers, often conversions from other warships. Germany partially completed one aircraft carrier, *Graf Zeppelin*, while the Italian aircraft carrier *Aquila*, almost ready for sea trials at the time of the armistice, also never became operational.

With the exception of the *Saipan* and *Independence* classes, built on heavy and light cruiser hulls, all American escort carriers (CVEs) were converted from merchant ship hulls, some of which were oilers/tankers, or purpose-built. For the British, Merchant Aircraft Carriers or MAC ships came into service in 1943, after the German prize *Hannover* had been converted into the carrier *Audacity* and proved the concept of the escort or auxiliary carrier. She had no hanger but carried four Martlets (US F4 Wildcats). Grain ships or tankers provided the hulls for MACs, still retaining at least three quarters of their capacity to carry cargo. Nineteen such carriers served, for which there are eight models, four based on grain ships and four on the tanker *Macoma*. Both of the MAC ship models in this chapter show bow A-frames for streaming paravanes to guard against mines. Conversions of the grain carriers had a

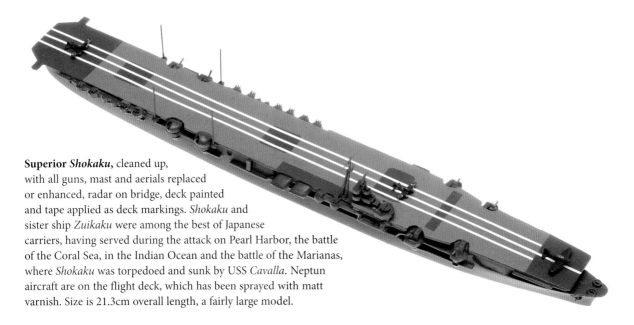

Superior *Shokaku*, cleaned up, with all guns, mast and aerials replaced or enhanced, radar on bridge, deck painted and tape applied as deck markings. *Shokaku* and sister ship *Zuikaku* were among the best of Japanese carriers, having served during the attack on Pearl Harbor, the battle of the Coral Sea, in the Indian Ocean and the battle of the Marianas, where *Shokaku* was torpedoed and sunk by USS *Cavalla*. Neptun aircraft are on the flight deck, which has been sprayed with matt varnish. Size is 21.3cm overall length, a fairly large model.

hanger while those of tankers did not, with their complement of four Swordfish biplanes having to be lashed down on the deck, with only wind screens for shelter. MAC ships provided an opportunity for aircraft to be recovered, but the slow Swordfish could only be submarine deterrents – although no submarines were sunk by these biplanes, no convoy with MACs lost any ships. British escort carriers also carried Martlets/ Wildcats, so these ships could provide both anti-aircraft and anti-submarine capability.

The USN had a total of sixty escort carriers while the RN had forty-five, of which thirty-nine were Lend-Lease. Britain designated her escort carriers either for anti-submarine or strike duty. Aircraft complements of the Allied escort carriers varied greatly: RN carriers, including MAC ships, had between four and twenty-four aircraft, which included Martlets, Swordfish, Fulmars, Fireflies, Sea Hurricanes, Avengers and Corsairs. The USN ships carried between twenty-eight and forty-eight aircraft, limited to FM2, F6F, F4U, TBM or TBFs. Thus the Allied navies had both ship types and at least three types of aircraft in common, although not all of the latter served on RN escort carriers. In some of the photographs here, numbers of the above aircraft are seen on the flight decks.

US escort carriers were highly effective in hunter-killer groups in the later stages of the Atlantic war, while in the Pacific, escort carriers supported the numerous amphibious operations against Japanese island bases and performed heroically in the battle off Samar during the larger campaign of Leyte Gulf, when 'Taffy 3' and its slim escort of destroyers and destroyer escorts fought off a vastly superior Japanese fleet of battleships, including the super battleship *Yamato*, cruisers and destroyers. Escort carriers had only one 5in gun each, while the escorting destroyers and destroyer escorts mounted a total of twenty-nine such guns, against the 18in weapons of the *Yamato*, but the concerted attacks of the carriers' Wildcats, Dauntless and Avengers, often without ordnance or ammunition, convinced the Japanese

Close-up of twin 5in and triple 25mm AA, with barrels replaced or cleaned up, and dapped and fabricated aluminium turrets placed over or near starboard turrets that are downwind of twin funnels; these turrets were to protect gun crews from noxious funnel smoke. Actual turrets were less round. Upper turrets are made in two parts, with a glued-on collar for the barrels to protrude through.

they were facing *Essex* class carriers, causing them to withdraw. The battle had a high cost for both sides, with three US escorts sunk, as well as the carriers *Gambier Bay* and *St. Lo*, while the Japanese lost three heavy cruisers.

Besides their historical importance, American escort carrier models represent a very full range of production techniques. These range from centrifugally-cast metal ships, using the European method of almost one-piece casting of models in rubber/silicone moulds, to the use of complex metal moulds for injection plastic models, which is a relatively rare manufacturing method for small-scale model ships, due to the high cost of the moulds and the relatively small market for such ships, in comparison to the larger hobby market for plastic models or kits. However, due to the need for injected plastic to be easily removed from the moulds, certain design features mar the look of some plastic models. If one looks closely at the

Superior *Shokaku*, a $20 used model with decals on flight deck and poor repair to aerials, otherwise stock, showing island and cast mast, beginning of enhancement, where portion of hull has been filed flat. Note that parts of the island have open spaces between decks. Given the gap between gun tubs/sponsons, it is most likely the flight deck was cast separately, as was the island. 5in and 25mm AA mounts are barely recognizable as guns.

Close-up of bridge and mast, *Shokaku*, late war, with Type 13 radar, and bedspring type radar on bridge. All AA gun barrels replaced with wire or enhanced by separating cast barrels, as can be seen by triple 25mm barrels on port side. Enhanced Neptun Zero by bridge, on hand-painted deck, where Scotch tape was used to mask elevators and other features which were not wood. Note downward-curved twin funnels aft of bridge, typical of Japanese carriers.

Covered AA mounts on starboard side aft of twin funnels. All radio aerials are drilled and glued onto their small round platforms. The hand-painted deck has Chartpak drafting tape applied to simulate deck markings, instead of decals, which I did not have. Images on the opposite page show steps in painting deck. When cast, 25mm AA were solid, not separate as shown here.

gun tubs of the HDS CVE *Casablanca*, the sides are not straight but curved inward, which greatly detracts from the accuracy but permits easier removal from the mould.

My modelling enhancements ranged from mild to fairly complex techniques. Many carrier enhancements are not dramatic, consisting of cleaning up the casting, correcting errors or replacing poorly-made AA guns. This usually involves serial fabrication of guns, then gluing on these tiny parts, an often difficult business. Most

aircraft carriers appear not to be cast in one piece; the Neptun *Empire Macrae* is a complex three-piece casting, even having a spring underneath the separate elevator, while the Oceanic *Audacity* is also a three-piece casting, with additionally a mast and A-frame for paravanes, missing from my used model but apparent from the paint scars of the missing pieces.

The Superior *Shokaku* involved much work, cleaning up the hull and areas where undercuts filled in, as well as enhancements to all AA guns,

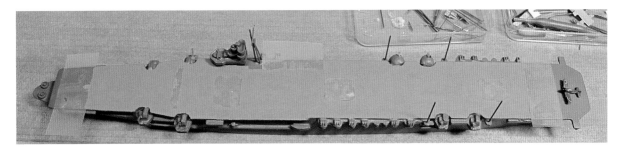

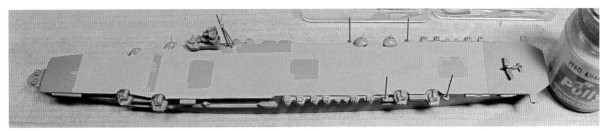

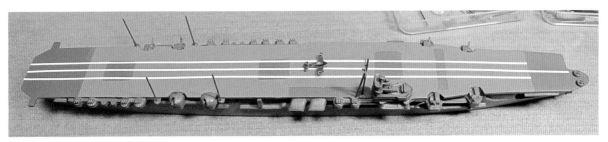

Masking of hand-painted deck and clean-up of finished and enhanced carrier *Shokaku*. Scotch tape was cut by hand to cover areas of deck not made of wood, represented by using Polly S Khaki. Note in first two photographs that paint has run under tape masks. Where this happened, sharp No.11 craft knife blades were used to scrape away the paint, then touched up with Tamiya Sasebo grey acrylic paint. The flight deck and hull were sprayed with matt varnish.

the mast and aerials, as well as masking the deck to show areas that were not wood. Similarly, the Superior *Sangamon*, a re-casting of the Framburg version, required much enhancement, with the cluster of bow 20mm gun tubs replaced by silver soldered metal tubing, the 5in gun sponsons cleaned up and the poorly-cast guns replaced with modified plastic 1/700 40mm guns. The islands were improved with yards and radar, and a catapult grooved into the deck. These additions were easy, yet really added to the realism of escort carriers. Because these ship models carried so many medium and light AA guns, enhancing such weapons was the most difficult job, and this makes the Neptun models stand out in quality, as this producer puts considerable effort into making accurate turrets, guns and AA weapons. In addition, the stenciled deck markings of Neptun and Hai carriers are difficult to duplicate for a modeller, usually requiring decals, often not readily available.

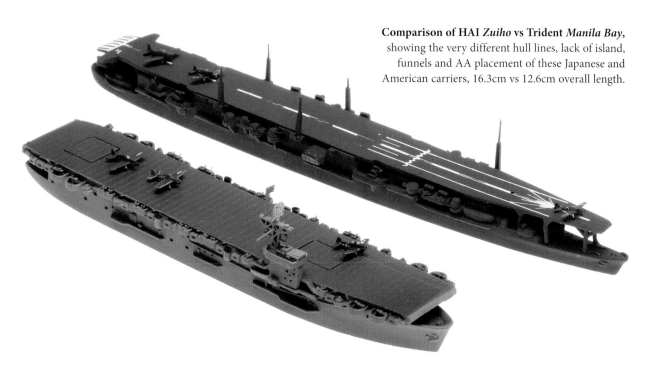

Comparison of HAI *Zuiho* vs Trident *Manila Bay*, showing the very different hull lines, lack of island, funnels and AA placement of these Japanese and American carriers, 16.3cm vs 12.6cm overall length.

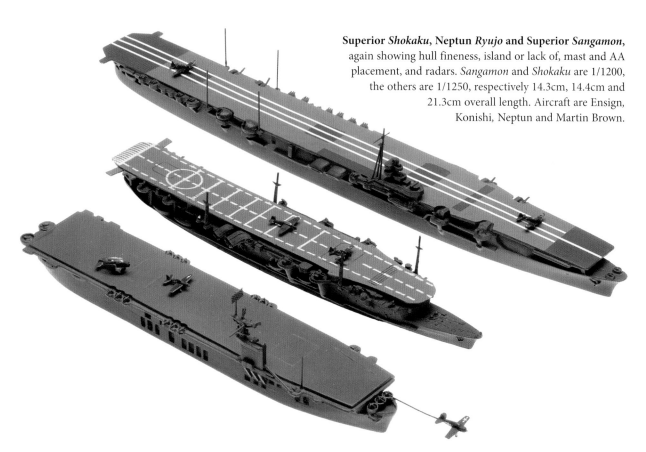

Superior *Shokaku*, Neptun *Ryujo* and Superior *Sangamon*, again showing hull fineness, island or lack of, mast and AA placement, and radars. *Sangamon* and *Shokaku* are 1/1200, the others are 1/1250, respectively 14.3cm, 14.4cm and 21.3cm overall length. Aircraft are Ensign, Konishi, Neptun and Martin Brown.

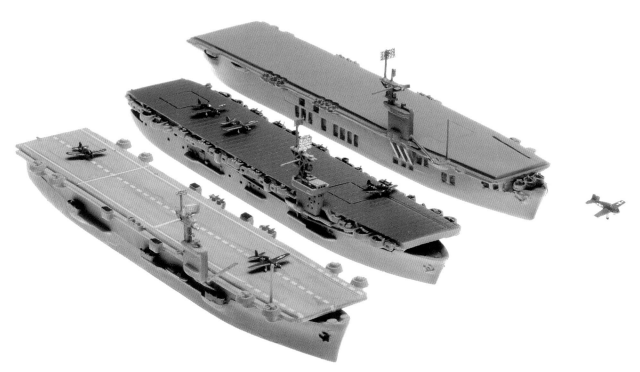

Comparison of Superior *Sangamon*, Trident Alpha *Manila Bay* and HDS/Schlingelhof *Casablanca*, with the *Sangamon* class being the only escort carriers in USN converted from oilers. The *Sangamon* is enhanced, the others almost stock. The dark deck of the *Manila Bay* shows the type of dark stain used by the USN on wood decks of escort carriers. *Sangamon* has Neptun Wildcat on wire to simulate being just launched.

Escort carriers and MAC ships. Hai *Pretoria Castle*, Superior *Sangamon*, Trident Alpha *Manila Bay*, HDS *Casablanca*, Wiking *Biter*, Hai *Empire MacAlpine* and Neptun *Empire MacRae*, latter two are British MAC ships. *Biter* and *Casablanca* are plastic injection moulded, rest cast metal; *Sangamon* is 1/1200, rest 1/1250. Escort carriers were important for convoy escort, anti-submarine (ASW) and local support of amphibious landings, 10.8cm to 14.6cm overall length. Note narrowness of flight decks on MAC ships, in comparison with Swordfish. The *Pretoria Castle*, *Sangamon* and *Biter* are all enhanced. Compared to British escort carriers, American ones were all broader in beam, a contrast also noticeable compared with the fine lines of the Japanese vessels opposite.

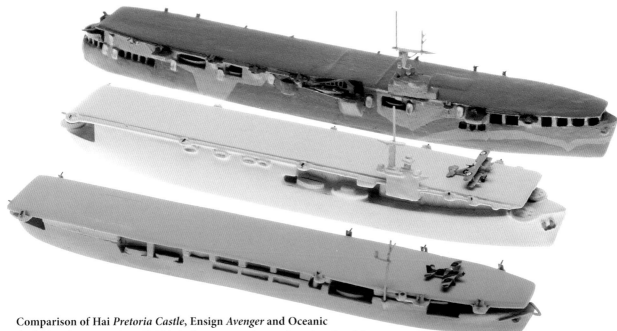

**Comparison of Hai *Pretoria Castle*, Ensign *Avenger* and Oceanic
Audacity,** demonstrating a British-built escort carrier, an American Lend-Lease
escort carrier (note quad 40mm in bow, taken from Framburg models) and the first British escort
carrier, converted from the German prize *Hannover*. She has no island, but does have a bridge
underneath the flight deck, and a paravane holder. Of these three models, the *Pretoria Castle*
required the most enhancement, followed by *Audacity;* models are 12.2cm to 14.6cm overall length.

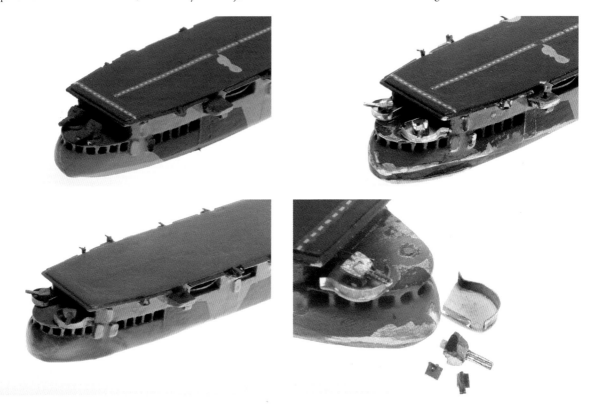

Hai *Pretoria Castle,* after enhancements, including bulwark at bow and the forward deck supports drilled out hollow, instead of previous solid casting. All sponsons have single or twin 20mm, seen in close-up on bottom right of opposite page. Mast now close to original, and cast crane now fabricated from aluminium sheet. Dimples in casting filled with Bondo.

Left: stages in correction of stern 4in mounts of *Pretoria Castle.* Upper left shows original, with mounts on stern deck, close to each other. Upper right shows the mounts cleaned and mounted on sponsons, as well as single 20mm made up of wire pedestal, aluminium shield and brass wire barrel. Bondo and plastic sheet added to level up stern by 1mm or more. Lower left shows repainted model, in colours used originally by Brian Vota. Bill Werner compared details with the excellent Sea Vee *Pretoria Castle* so I could determine correct placement of guns, although the Hai model does not have all the required sponsons. Lower right shows close-up of mounted twin 4in in overhanging sponson, loose mount, sponson, single and twin 20mm AA. Gun tub formed, then glued to thin yellow plastic. When dry, excess plastic was filed away, and opening cut in shield for gun crew access.

Three British escort carriers were recently acquired by the author, made by Ensign, Hai and Oceanic; all were rather poor models, especially in terms of their armament. Some even lacked correct gun positions, while in others the guns/mounts were so poorly modelled and cast as to defy identification. To correct such deficiencies requires much work, since aircraft carriers mounted so many AA guns and the mounts or sponsons are so small that it forces the ship modeller to simplify. Later in this chapter, I show the single and twin 20mm AA guns for HMS *Pretoria Castle*, as an example of small and simplified weapons. With cast models, it is also difficult to reproduce the complex and delicate masts, which really need to be fabricated from thin wire to achieve an accurate representation.

Every aircraft carrier model needs aircraft to complete its appearance, and this also adds much due to the contrasting colour and size of these tiny models on a deck, giving that busy look which adds to realism for all ship models. All my aircraft are enhanced by filing to thin wings and correct configuration, and painted and decaled, each requiring appreciable work. Some are fitted with guns, radar and the like.

Both Allied and Axis carriers were often camouflaged, sometimes in a bizarre manner, such as giant painted turrets on the flight deck of a Japanese carrier. Even less complicated camouflage schemes are difficult to do well, and it is especially hard to match colours when doing a restoration. I have left mine largely in the paint schemes of the producers, except for the *Shokaku*. British carriers usually had two to four-colour camouflage, although MAC ships were one colour. HMS *Avenger* had a complicated flight deck camouflage. While USN carriers were often camouflaged, their flight decks were not.

Since I am interested in the comparative approach to naval ship model collecting and enhancement, I am particularly engaged with escort carriers, since their models differ so much in level of modelling and detail, and are a real challenge to correct for accuracy.

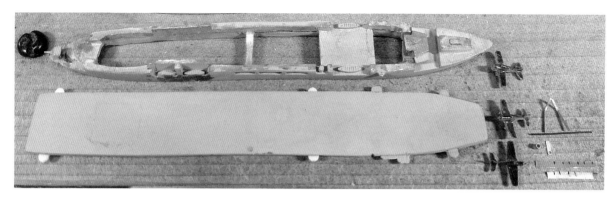

Above: **Oceanic *Audacity* prior to assembly,** showing the three-part casting of hull, bridge (partially unpainted structure in well-deck) and flight deck. White plastic sponsons have been glued on Single 4in at stern has been enhanced, with correct mount shape and breech. Adjacent are Ensign and Neptun Grumman F4s/Martlets, before repainting. Note paravane made from lead alloy sprue, iron wire for mast, parts for mast and small tub by mast as well as aluminium sheet with saw cuts for serial fabrication of the AA guns. Original model had no guns except that at the stern. There is conflicting information on how many 20mm and 40mm weapons she had. I did not differentiate between the two types and the number of sponsons might not be correct. The best reference is a 1/300 model in the Merseyside Maritime Museum, and this was what I followed.

Below and right: **Comparison of Hai *Pretoria Castle,* Ensign *Avenger,* Wiking *Biter,* Oceanic *Audacity,* Neptun *Empire MacAlpine* and Hai *Empire MacRae,*** showing the variety of escort carriers employed by the RN. Except for MAC ships, all British escort carriers were camouflaged; some, like *Avenger,* even had the landing deck fully camouflaged. The Wiking *Biter* is plastic injected; I drilled out the starboard side and enhanced the guns on that side, but left the port side. Right-hand image shows close-ups of the *Pretoria Castle, Avenger* and *Audacity*: note differences in British and US islands, and no island on *Audacity.*

13

SUPERIOR *KONGO* AND *MOGAMI*

Ship modellers work on a variety of models differing in quality. Most of my experience has been with those derived from WWII recognition models. Usually, I do not try to enhance an actual recognition model, preserving it as a historic document, but work on second-generation models, like those produced by Superior. These are much less expensive, especially if used, so less caution is required than when working on, for example, a German Neptun model. Often, enhancements greatly improve such models, making them worthwhile for any collection. Sometimes, a little more effort results in a unique model, such as the *Kongo* and *Mogami* shown here, with the Japanese practice of aerial towers on gun turrets.

Because models originally based on recognition ones are usually cast in one piece, except for the main-battery, they often require a good deal of cleaning up, as spaces between structures once cast separately tend to fill up with metal. The captions describe the amount of enhancements done to *Kongo* and *Mogami*; the battleship fought off Samar against 'Taffy 3', and the heavy cruiser at the battle of Surigao Strait. While both Japanese ships are in late-war guise, their light AA is inaccurate, as by 1944-5 the number of 25mm AA guns were so numerous that until recently (by PaperLab) no producer in small scales has made an entirely accurate model regarding this.

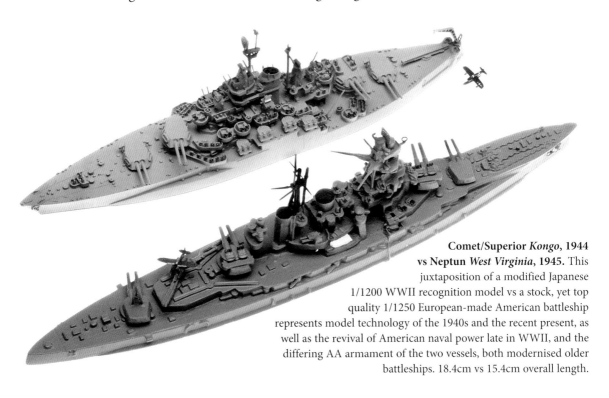

Comet/Superior *Kongo*, 1944 vs Neptun *West Virginia*, 1945. This juxtaposition of a modified Japanese 1/1200 WWII recognition model vs a stock, yet top quality 1/1250 European-made American battleship represents model technology of the 1940s and the recent present, as well as the revival of American naval power late in WWII, and the differing AA armament of the two vessels, both modernised older battleships. 18.4cm vs 15.4cm overall length.

Enhanced Superior *Kongo*, showing extensive modifications to bridge, with additions to gun director, radar, navigation radio aerial, yards, as well as mainmast. Superstructure of bridge has been hollowed out with drills and burrs, gun barrels separated where possible. Note that mainmast above the level of the funnel tops is painted black so smoke stains do not show. Most of the modifications were done a decade ago, so they are not at my current level of detail. Lower right image shows installation of copper/steel wire aerial tower on 'Y' turret.

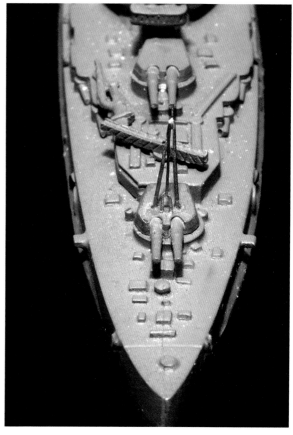

Comparison of wartime recognition Comet *Mogami* and enhanced *Mogami*, showing the improvements made by Superior, and the enhancements I made of soldered turret aerials, masts, yards, radar, 'Pete' floatplane and funnel. Recognition model is screwed to wood plinth; I always remove the wood so that acids in it do not attack the metal alloy. Image below shows Superior model prior to enhancements, though with some clean-up of the masts, which may have been soldered. In comparison the photograph overleaf shows the enhanced model with the trunked funnels now separated. Comet *Mogami* is 19.0cm overall length.

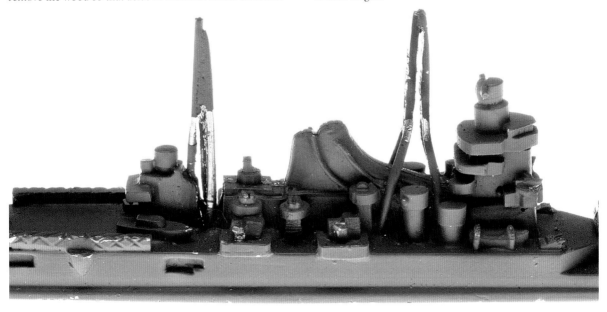

Enhanced Superior *Mogami*, based on a wartime Comet recognition model. Comparison with previous original model shows that Superior had already enhanced the model with anchor chains, better 5in mounts and addition of 25mm AA mountings. The original recognition model apparently lacked masts and I am not certain if the aircraft crane was correct. I have added detail to both masts, including radar and a slightly different crane. Japanese bedspring-type radars always have a thick frame, versus none on US bedspring-type radar. The *Mogami* has aerial towers on 'C' and 'X' turrets. The faired funnels have now been drilled, pierced so that a triangular space separates them, probably not possible when the wartime recognition model was centrifugally cast in a hard rubber mould, due to the problem with undercuts. To be accurate, this heavy cruiser would have had many more multiple and single 25mm AA, the latter never modelled on any US recognition models. Note the 'Pete' floatplane on catapult.

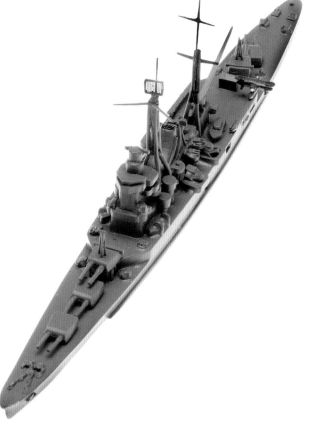

14

EIJO MARU, RARE MODEL

In 2012, I bid on German eBay for two Japanese naval ship models made by the late P. Otten, with the help of a German friend. Otten was Russian and a fairly prolific maker of resin ships, as his friend Anton Kozhevnikov told me, who inherited the entire Otten collection. One was a WWII *Maru* that had been mounted with 18th century guns, which I believe was a joke. After removing these, cleaning up and repainting it, I sold it at the San Pedro meeting of the SMSC, the primary US small ship model collectors' group. These models were painted a very dark grey,

which also made it difficult to determine if they were well made. At first glance, the ships looked decent, especially when seen on the Internet; but when examined closely, they were poorly cast, especially with details like armament, and not accurate compared to the originals. The hulls were very rough and bulwarks were not always complete. The model that interested me the most was the IJN's *Eijo Maru*, launched in 1944 as a Type 2DRS Standard Freighter of over 3,000 tons, requisitioned at the beginning of 1945 as a minelayer and completed in March. She was sunk

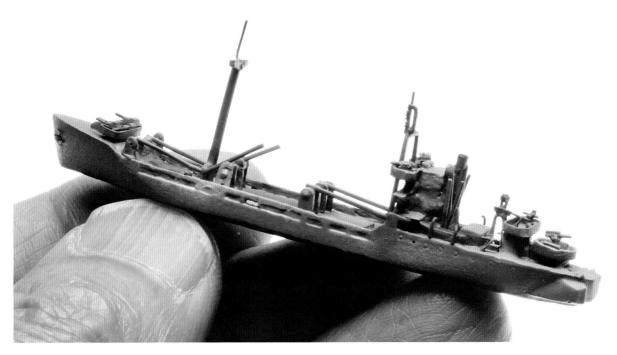

Reworked and restored *Eijo Maru*, a late-war Japanese auxiliary minelayer, converted from one of their five Standard Freighter types. Of resin, and only 7.2cm long, she is armed with a stern 3in gun, two triple 25mm at the bow, two double 25mm on the bridge and four single 25mm aft. The three sets of structures near the bow and amidships are mine lifts. Detailing included a radar on the bridge and a search-light platform aft, although the stern gun barrel is too short.

in June by USS *Spadefish*, so I am not certain if she ever laid any mines. She would have been useful in laying defensive minefields in an attempt to keep US submarines out of the Inland Sea. There are small scale models of some of the five types of Japanese standard freighters and tanker types set up in 1942, somewhat like the 'Liberty' and 'Victory' ships of the US, but none shown as converted to an auxiliary minelayer. The ships were coal-fired, but still capable of 10–11 knots,

(some, like the standardised tankers, were faster) and all were designed to be built quickly.

In the photo on this page, I lightened the original colour to better show the features of the model as bought, for €29. Due to the rarity of this model, I felt it was worthwhile to rework it as accurately as possible; the image on the previous page shows the restored/reworked ship before the stern gun was corrected. Since there are no drawings for *Eijo Maru*, I based my model on her sister

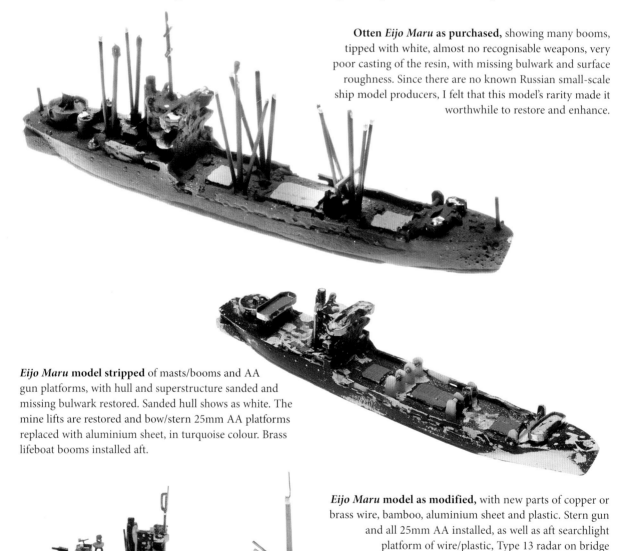

Otten *Eijo Maru* as purchased, showing many booms, tipped with white, almost no recognisable weapons, very poor casting of the resin, with missing bulwark and surface roughness. Since there are no known Russian small-scale ship model producers, I felt that this model's rarity made it worthwhile to restore and enhance.

Eijo Maru **model stripped** of masts/booms and AA gun platforms, with hull and superstructure sanded and missing bulwark restored. Sanded hull shows as white. The mine lifts are restored and bow/stern 25mm AA platforms replaced with aluminium sheet, in turquoise colour. Brass lifeboat booms installed aft.

Eijo Maru **model as modified,** with new parts of copper or brass wire, bamboo, aluminium sheet and plastic. Stern gun and all 25mm AA installed, as well as aft searchlight platform of wire/plastic, Type 13 radar on bridge mast and copper anchors at bow.

ship, *Minoo Maru*, also available as a metal model by Yorck. While fitted out as minelayers, they could still be used for carrying freight when the holds were empty of mines.

I stripped the model of all masts/booms and AA gun platforms, sanded the hull and superstructure and restored the missing bulwark. I also restored the mine lifts and installed AA gun platforms of aluminium sheet and plastic, as well as a pair of copper wires aft for the lifeboat booms. The mine lifts and bulwark are made of styrene sheet. Such mine lifts are similar to those on the Neptun or Trident minelayers. The modified model has new parts made of copper or brass wire, bamboo, aluminium sheet and plastic. The overhead view demonstrates how much of the model has been modified or replaced, including the anchor winch, cargo winches, anchors, weapons, booms, masts and mine lifts. The copper wire for the booms has been slightly forged so that they are flattened, and 26-gauge copper wire used for 25mm AA gun barrels. Ready-ammo bins have been placed near almost all the guns. The turquoise colour is from aluminium quick print plates, one of the most useful materials for small-scale ship modelling. The close-up of the stern shows single 25mm guns and their magazines, searchlight platform and bridge structures. Note the mine chutes, which were partially restored. The completed model is 7.2cm overall length. After the model was finished, I realised the barrel of the stern gun was too short,

Eijo Maru, **showing sanded areas as white resin;** note the numerous white dimples, each a raised dot on the badly-cast resin hull. Mine lifts are white styrene, as well as replacement bulwark. Brass and copper wire used for fabricating anchors, winches, booms, mine lifts and 25mm AA barrels. Turquoise aluminium sheet was used for AA platforms and shields. Note much of aluminium sheet was sanded to square it off, thus the loss of colour. Type 13 radar is of blue plastic sprue. Stern gun tub was the original cast resin, but thinned out with burrs. The forward boom mast is of bamboo, a good material for scratch-building, as it is strong, light in weight and is easy to smooth.

Close-up view of stern, showing extensive modifications. Note Japanese AA shields tend to be squared or with chamfered corners, and not round as with most other navies. *Eijo Maru* had single, double and triple 25mm AA guns. Single guns have white plastic magazines and a very distinctive goose-neck mount; the guns were derived from a Hotchkiss design.

so it was replaced with a longer one. Larger 1/700 plastic models do show rails running from the forward mine lift to the bridge, so the mines most likely ran on rails to the stern mine chutes, via openings below the bridge. There is a poor extant photograph of a lateral view of *Minoo Maru*, as well as very good lateral and stern view drawings of this ship in Fukui's very useful *Japanese Naval Vessels at the End of World War II*. In the late Pacific war,

most Japanese ships engaged by US forces were small, like guard or picket boats, sea trucks and auxiliaries like *Eijo Maru*, and these are usually ignored by model producers. Japan, an island nation, used numerous small ships/boats for both commerce and as auxiliary warships. Harms' ONI CD (see Bibliography) shows well all the types of these small vessels employed by the Japanese Navy, and is very useful for ship modellers.

Overhead view of *Eijo Maru*, now painted a dark grey. She is heavily armed, a reflection of the great threat of US naval aircraft late in the Pacific war. Note the stern mine chutes, seen as bulges. In the actual vessel, mine rails ran to the bridge, and then to the two stern mine chutes.

***Eijo Maru* after completion,** clearly showing the mine lifts, as modelled by both Neptun and Trident. The actual ones were more lattice-work in appearance, as shown in a photo of *Minoo*, and in drawings by Fukui of her sister ship in *Japanese Naval Vessels at the End of World War II*. The booms were for cargo handling when she was not engaged in mine-laying and was used as a freighter. When fully loaded, these ships displaced 5,200 tons.

***Eijo Maru* with corrected longer stern gun.** Although an auxiliary minelayer, she has three cargo hatches and booms to service them, so she would most likely still be able to carry cargo, fulfilling a dual function. Painted with Tamiya Kure grey.

15

TAMANO, 'NEVER WAS' SHIP

The Japanese Navy often designed ships with a dual purpose, or so that they could be easily converted from one use to another, such as seaplane carriers into aircraft carriers. The Martin Brown model in this chapter is a 'never was' ship, often of interest to collectors. *Tamano*, incorrectly labelled *Takano* by the manufacturer, was one of a class of seven cancelled high-speed oilers and aircraft transports with catapults. A similar ship, the *Hayasui*, with one catapult and six aircraft, was

MB Models (Martin Brown)/Highworth 1/1250 'IJNS *Takano*' instruction sheet, model label, colour photograph of finished model and components of kit spread out. Photo-etch of brass; hull and parts were probably of spin-cast lead alloy. Overall length of model, obtained in 2011, is 12.5cm. Nine cast 'Kate' torpedo bombers are supplied, of the total of fourteen designed to be carried.

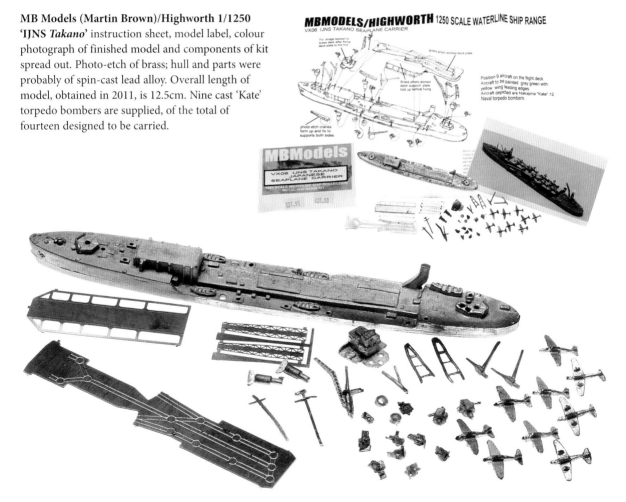

View of hull, as well as cast and photo-etched parts. Mounting holes have been pre-drilled. I used additional brass rods and copper wire/iron wire for the booms and gun barrels, only after considerable cleaning-up of the parts. 26-gauge copper wire was used for replacing all of the 25mm barrels.

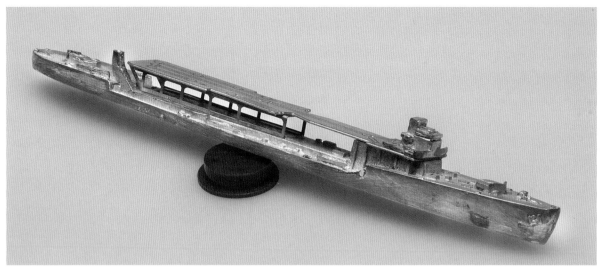

Canted view of hull and installed photo-etched aircraft deck: hull filled and filed.

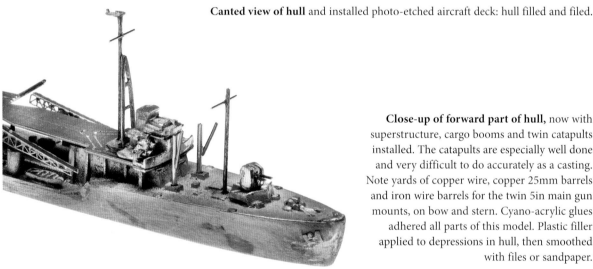

Close-up of forward part of hull, now with superstructure, cargo booms and twin catapults installed. The catapults are especially well done and very difficult to do accurately as a casting. Note yards of copper wire, copper 25mm barrels and iron wire barrels for the twin 5in main gun mounts, on bow and stern. Cyano-acrylic glues adhered all parts of this model. Plastic filler applied to depressions in hull, then smoothed with files or sandpaper.

Close-up view of stern, with the cast aircraft crane now drilled out, adding realism, as cranes were normally latticework to decrease weight. Part of aft mast has been replaced by brass rod, and triple barrels of 25mm AA and stern 5in guns replaced. Space under photo-etched deck was for storage of additional aircraft.

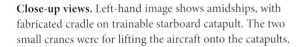

Close-up views. Left-hand image shows amidships, with fabricated cradle on trainable starboard catapult. The two small cranes were for lifting the aircraft onto the catapults, while the large crane at the stern was for lifting aircraft onto the ship. The right-hand image shows the bridge, triple 25mm AA and bow 5in guns, with the mounting enhanced.

completed in 1944 but was sunk later that same year by a US submarine.

While I do not collect 'never was' models, this MB kit was one of a very few that had extensive photo-etched parts, with the rest cast in lead alloy. With good, clear instructions, and nine 'Kate' torpedo bombers, there were many cast parts. The brass photo-etched structures were easily bent into shape and installed on the model, but the hull, superstructure and other cast parts needed a good deal of cleaning up and enhancement, the armament in particular, because Japanese gun turrets and AA guns are very distinctive. This kit clearly demonstrates how photo-etched parts add to the accuracy and attractiveness of a ship model.

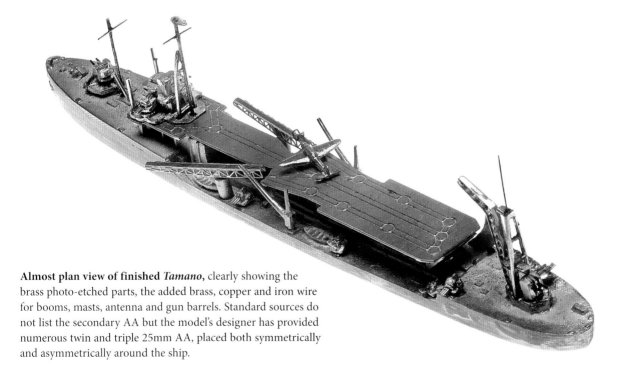

Almost plan view of finished *Tamano*, clearly showing the brass photo-etched parts, the added brass, copper and iron wire for booms, masts, antenna and gun barrels. Standard sources do not list the secondary AA but the model's designer has provided numerous twin and triple 25mm AA, placed both symmetrically and asymmetrically around the ship.

16

US AND JAPANESE TRANSPORTS AND ESCORTS

Much of the Pacific naval war in WWII involved logistics: for the Japanese it was keeping supply lines open, while for the Allies it was supporting the task forces engaged in amphibious operations capturing Japanese island bases. These types of operations required large numbers of transports and cargo ships, together with their escorts. While Japanese amphibious landings early in the war involved up to forty-three transports, Allied landings later in the war numbered hundreds of ships. Only recently has a model been made of a Japanese equivalent of an

APA with accurate AA, the Spider Navy SN 2-14 *Yasukawa Maru*, here compared to the Neptun APA 33 *Bayfield*, with both carrying landing craft as deck cargo. *Yasukawa Maru* was one of nine ships converted by the Japanese Army into AA ships or *Bokusens*, though later reverting to a transport role as AA armament on merchant ships was increased. As such ships always required escorts, I have included in this chapter American destroyers, destroyer escorts and their Japanese equivalents, destroyers and *Kaibokans*. Escorts are fascinating models to collect, given their vital role

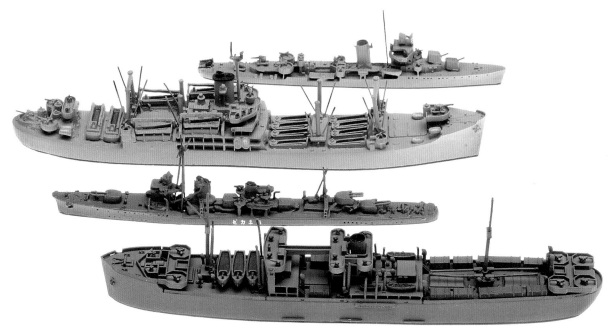

Neptun APA 33 *Bayfield*, Albatros destroyer *Kearney* vs Spider Navy *Yasukawa Maru* and Optatus destroyer *Hatsukaze*. The APA was a damaged model, now restored and paint re-touched, whereas all the others are stock. They range between 9.5cm and 12.1cm overall length. Note elaborate AA platforms for *Yasukawa Maru* and that it carries three well-modelled *daihatsus*, with shields for steering positions.

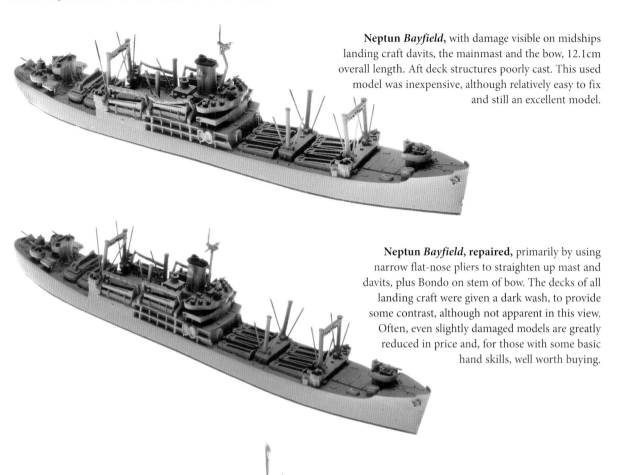

Neptun *Bayfield*, with damage visible on midships landing craft davits, the mainmast and the bow, 12.1cm overall length. Aft deck structures poorly cast. This used model was inexpensive, although relatively easy to fix and still an excellent model.

Neptun *Bayfield*, repaired, primarily by using narrow flat-nose pliers to straighten up mast and davits, plus Bondo on stem of bow. The decks of all landing craft were given a dark wash, to provide some contrast, although not apparent in this view. Often, even slightly damaged models are greatly reduced in price and, for those with some basic hand skills, well worth buying.

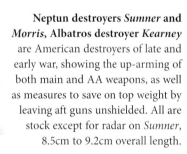

Neptun destroyers *Sumner* and *Morris*, Albatros destroyer *Kearney* are American destroyers of late and early war, showing the up-arming of both main and AA weapons, as well as measures to save on top weight by leaving aft guns unshielded. All are stock except for radar on *Sumner*, 8.5cm to 9.2cm overall length.

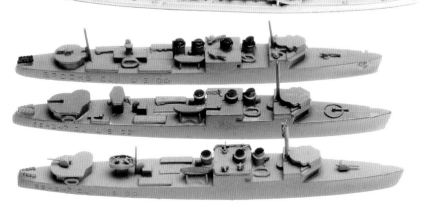

Comet destroyer *Brooks*, '66-347' classes of flush-deck destroyers; *Brooks* with four funnels, stock. Middle model stock, poorly modelled open main guns; lower model with turreted guns, enhanced with light AA, both 7.8cm overall length, with three cut-down funnels, vs four on *Brooks*, still in WWI configuration, 7.9cm overall length.

Framburg *Rudderow*, Neptun *Rudderow*, *Buckley*, *Cannon* and frigate *Tacoma*, 7.5cm to 7.8cm overall length, all destroyer escorts with 5in/38 or 3in main-battery, 40mm and 20mm AA, except *Buckley* with quad 1.1in aft, rarely seen in models. Framburg *Rudderow* is die-cast zinc, with less detailed 40mm but otherwise excellent ID model. Note 1/1200 Framburg has torpedo tubes, while Neptun *Rudderow* has additional 40mm and 20mm instead.

Japanese anti-aircraft destroyers *Terutsuki* vs Neptun *Akitsuki*, with *Terutsuki* completely rebuilt, while early-war *Akitsuki* has copper torpedo crane, plastic crow's nest and copper yards. Both ships were armed with the excellent 3.9in gun. Models are 10.8cm overall length.

in all navies, as well as their variety, as shown by the images here. Especially interesting are Japanese destroyers, many of which were extremely effective in torpedo attacks during the Pacific war, being armed with powerful 24in oxygen-powered 'Long Lance' torpedoes. Maru's *Mechanisms of Japanese Destroyers* is a very detailed and useful book on Japanese destroyers and destroyer escorts.

Superior *Kagero* vs *Matsu*. Both models have been enhanced, with Japanese Type 13 and 22 radars now fitted on *Matsu*, Japan's version of the US destroyer escort.

Along with the *Kaibokans*, these were badly-needed escorts during the mid- and late Pacific war. Models are 8.9cm to 10.0cm overall length.

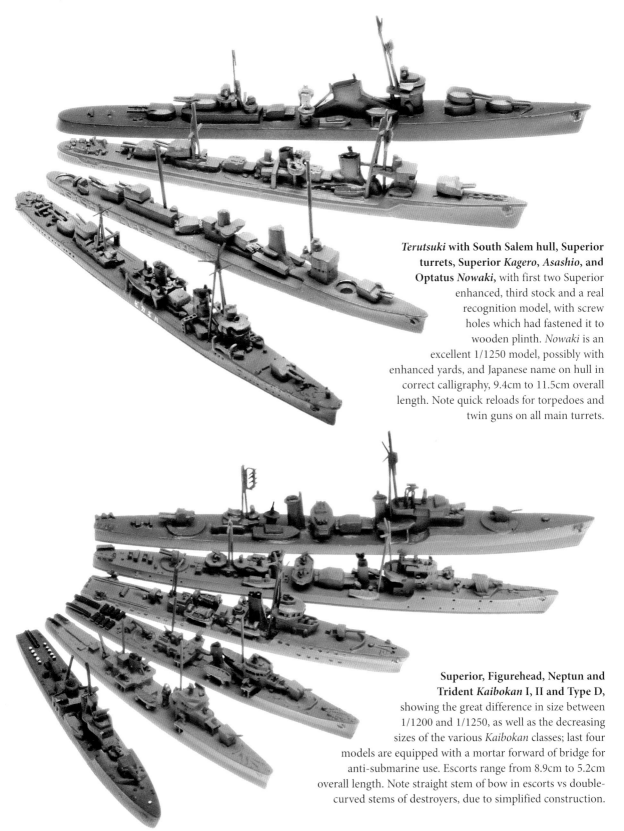

Terutsuki **with South Salem hull, Superior turrets, Superior** *Kagero*, *Asashio*, **and Optatus** *Nowaki*, with first two Superior enhanced, third stock and a real recognition model, with screw holes which had fastened it to wooden plinth. *Nowaki* is an excellent 1/1250 model, possibly with enhanced yards, and Japanese name on hull in correct calligraphy, 9.4cm to 11.5cm overall length. Note quick reloads for torpedoes and twin guns on all main turrets.

Superior, Figurehead, Neptun and Trident *Kaibokan* **I, II and Type D,** showing the great difference in size between 1/1200 and 1/1250, as well as the decreasing sizes of the various *Kaibokan* classes; last four models are equipped with a mortar forward of bridge for anti-submarine use. Escorts range from 8.9cm to 5.2cm overall length. Note straight stem of bow in escorts vs double-curved stems of destroyers, due to simplified construction.

17

HOKOKU MARU, BENGAL AND ONDINA

One of the most unequal naval engagements of WWII was the late 1942 battle in the Indian Ocean between the Dutch Shell tanker *Ondina*, the Royal Indian Navy minesweeper *Bengal* and two Japanese AMCs, the *Hokoku Maru* and *Aikoku Maru*. Besides 20mm AA, *Ondina* had an American 4in gun (with only forty shells) on the stern, and *Bengal* a 12pdr, against the AMCs, each of which had eight 5.5in guns, plus 76mm, 25mm and 13mm AA, two twin torpedo tubes and two floatplanes. While *Ondina* steamed away, *Bengal* moved forward to engage the enemy. Both Allied vessels fired at the Japanese, and a lucky shot from *Ondina* hit the port torpedo tube of *Hokoku Maru*, which exploded, resulting in a series of fires and explosions that sank her. Although both Allied ships were damaged, with *Ondina* torpedoed, abandoned and re-boarded, both escaped when *Aikoku Maru* stopped to rescue her sister ship's crew. This battle well demonstrates how courage and luck can play a major role in war.

If a ship or aircraft model is to undergo modification or restoration, it should always be photographed before work begins, as documentation. Since there was so much conflicting information on the ships involved in this battle, I gathered all that was available into an illustrated document. After printout, the pages were punched and put into a three-ring workshop binder, so the information could be accessed when I was at my model-making bench.

Only recently have models of *Hokoku Maru* been made, by both CMP and Hai, the latter

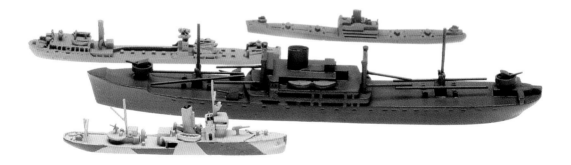

Ondina and *Bengal* vs *Hokoku Maru* and *Aikoku Maru*: to represent this battle, I converted the Argonaut 914 *Bathurst* class minesweeper into HMIS *Bengal* (4.8cm overall length); this involved rebuilding the model from a ship with three turrets, two sited forward, into one with an unshielded forward 12pdr gun and three 20mm, as well as other major structural changes. An Authenticast 1/1200 Japanese freighter was converted to an AMC (similar to *Saigon* or *Bangkok Maru* with four main guns) and two 1/2400 ships were used, with the difference in scale to give a forced perspective. The 1/2400 Sea Battle tanker is much more heavily armed than the real *Ondina* while the 1/1200 and 1/2400 Japanese freighters are much less well-armed than the actual Japanese AMCs *Hokoku Maru* and *Aikoku Maru*.

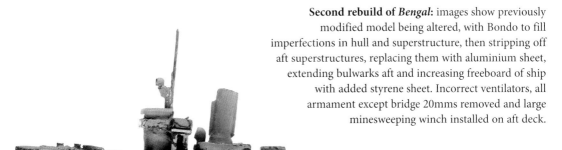

Second rebuild of *Bengal*: images show previously modified model being altered, with Bondo to fill imperfections in hull and superstructure, then stripping off aft superstructures, replacing them with aluminium sheet, extending bulwarks aft and increasing freeboard of ship with added styrene sheet. Incorrect ventilators, all armament except bridge 20mms removed and large minesweeping winch installed on aft deck.

Rebuilt *Bengal*, now with four correct ventilators carved from plastic sprue, yards on masts, as well as jack staff. Cranes and lifeboat davits installed; crow's nest, searchlight and anchors added and bow and stern guns reworked. Stern gun has been described as 40mm Bofors by some, but more likely a 2pdr pom-pom, given the scarcity of the Swedish gun in early WWII. Hull is changed and increased in depth,

as was characteristic of the *Bathurst* class, and bulwark extends almost to stern. Bondo was applied to all areas that needed fill; this automotive product is excellent for ship modelling, and inexpensive, with a long shelf life. Lower image shows painted *Bengal*, in white and black; bow gun was black, as verified by a wartime film, and mostly follows Wright's *British and Commonwealth Warship Camouflage*.

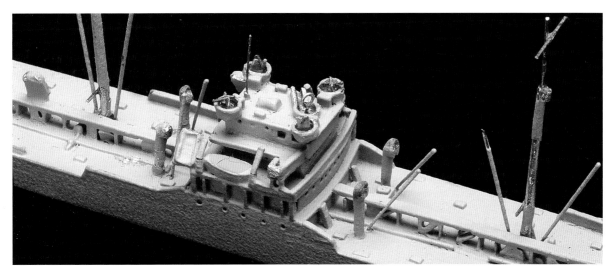

Stock and modified CMP *Ondina*: Dutch tanker still in carton, showing incorrect stern guns, poorly cast structures such as ventilators, bent ladder, 20mm AA and cracking paint on lifeboats. Bottom photograph shows Bondo repairs before sanding, addition of antenna/yards, replacement of all four 20mm AA with wire barrels, aluminium shields and radio loop, and thinner antenna on bridge. Paint is chipping on derricks, although generally features on this model are detailed and good. *Ondina* is 10.8cm overall length. I strongly believe that ships which took part in heroic battles should be honoured with accuracy if modelled.

mastered by John Youngerman. Each is different and neither is completely accurate. In order to show the ships involved in this historic battle, I ordered the Hai AMC and the CMP *Ondina*, and extensively rebuilt my previously altered *Bengal*. The Dutch tanker had only minor alterations, the main one in having two stern guns instead of one. Omissions or too much incorrect armament is a continuing problem with small-scale ship models. The *Hokoku Maru* needed much work to make her accurate enough, although I am not sure if she carried a second false funnel at the time of the battle, and there is a lot of discrepancy between the camouflage schemes carried by her and her sister ship *Aikoku Maru*, as seen in 1/700 plastic or 1/1250 metal models. Because of the interest in

Close-up of *Ondina* stern, now with only one 4in gun on upper poop deck, cleaned-up aft superstructure and wire/aluminium sheet shields for 20mm AA, paint touched up, including skylights on engine room. Incorrect second gun now removed from stern. The lucky shot from this ship hit the port torpedo of *Hokoku Maru*, causing it to explode, thus setting the ship on fire, and later sinking. When sister AMC *Aikoku Maru* went to rescue survivors, the Dutch tanker and *Bengal* were able to escape, although both had been hit, the tanker by gunfire and three torpedoes.

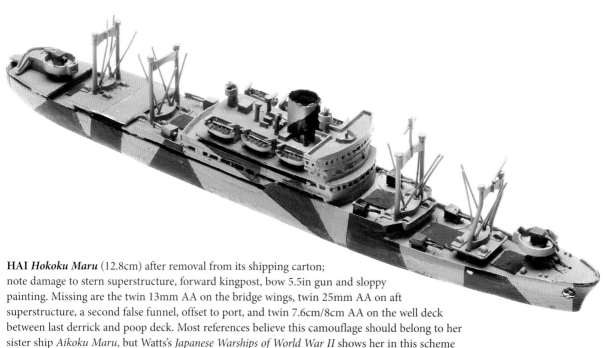

HAI *Hokoku Maru* (12.8cm) after removal from its shipping carton; note damage to stern superstructure, forward kingpost, bow 5.5in gun and sloppy painting. Missing are the twin 13mm AA on the bridge wings, twin 25mm AA on aft superstructure, a second false funnel, offset to port, and twin 7.6cm/8cm AA on the well deck between last derrick and poop deck. Most references believe this camouflage should belong to her sister ship *Aikoku Maru*, but Watts's *Japanese Warships of World War II* shows her in this scheme on July, 1942. The *CMP* model of this AMC has the bridge machine guns, but not other AA.

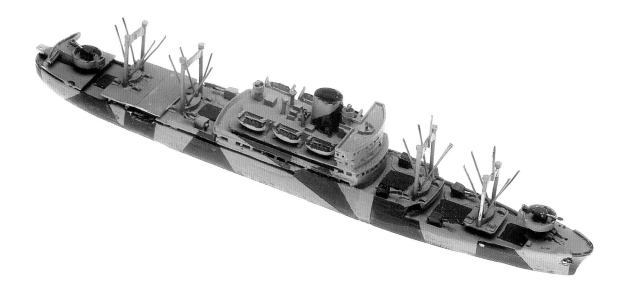

HAI *Hokoku Maru* corrections/enhancements in progress, with Bondo on poorly-cast parts of model, including 5.5in gun barrels. Note that the starboard torpedo position has been burred open, as otherwise the torpedoes cannot swing out and fire. Bent structures have been straightened. Bottom image shows corrections of additional masts/antenna on derricks or kingposts, bridge 13mm machine guns and rangefinder, two aft twin 25mm, second false funnel of plastic sprue, and raised AA platform for twin 76mm guns aft. All gun positions were supplied with ready-use ammunition boxes if space available. Because of extensive Bondo fill and sanding/filing of hull, almost entire hull and superstructure needed to have paint retouched. Enhancements involved plastic sprue, aluminium sheet, iron, copper and brass wire of varying thicknesses. All gluing was with 'New Glue', a long-lasting and thin cyano-acrylic glue used primarily by beaders/jewellers. One of the problems with doing corrections or enhancements is that once you start the process, more and more areas seem to need attention, to match those parts that have been corrected.

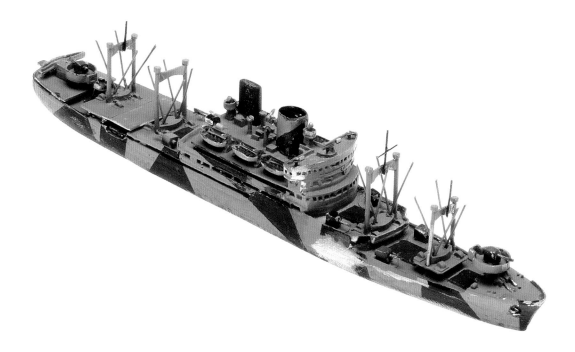

Close-ups of *Hokoku Maru* showing extensive modifications/additions to Hai model: mast/yard on forward derrick, dual 13mm AA on bridge wings, rangefinder on centre bridge, second false funnel, twin 25mm AA on aft superstructure, additional antenna on last derrick and twin 3in AA aft, on elevated platform. There are now cutouts for the torpedo tubes and Bondo has been applied to hull and other casting defects. Lower image shows close-up of ship with camouflage restored by masking with tape and using spray paint, with hand retouching and cleaning up. 'Jake' floatplane on aft deck, although 'Alfs' and 'Petes' were used.

this historic battle, many collectors have models of one or both Japanese AMCs; the CM *Hokoku Maru* is painted in overall grey, so one has to apply one's own *Hokoku Maru* or *Aikoku Maru* camouflage scheme. Youngerman must have based his paint scheme on the July 1942 photo of *Hokoku Maru* in Watts' *Japanese Warships of World War II* (1971), which is contrary to most of the fifteen paint schemes of *Hokoku Maru* and *Aikoku Maru* seen elsewhere, often on the Internet.

There is only one extant drawing of the *Hokoku Maru* that shows all the details I have added, except that the aft twin 76mm AA is missing. There is very little space between the aft end of the superstructure and the poop deck, so the AA platform is very small but the one available photograph of *Gokoku Maru*, the third sister ship, shows a similarly small AA platform. The gun tubs for the 76mm and 25mm AA are all square, usually with chamfered corners; the Japanese did not use round gun tubs except on their carriers.

It took a total of ninety-one partial days to correct and enhance the *Bengal*, *Ondina* and *Hokoku Maru* models featured in this chapter, not including time for research, laying out documentation and photographing the models in progress or finished. I usually worked in the morning before going to my office, then after dinner, often until late. If a collector does not engage in enhancements or conversions of models, they may not realise how much time is required to do such work. Rebuilding the *Bengal* and restoring the camouflage scheme of the Japanese AMC required the most time, especially in the never-ending retouching of paint, which sometimes obscured details on the models. Of course, it is the challenge and the ultimate satisfaction of being able to really produce a miniature representation of history that keeps one devoting so much time and effort to such models. If a ship or aircraft model is incorrect, I would rather not have it in my collection, not unless it can be made accurate.

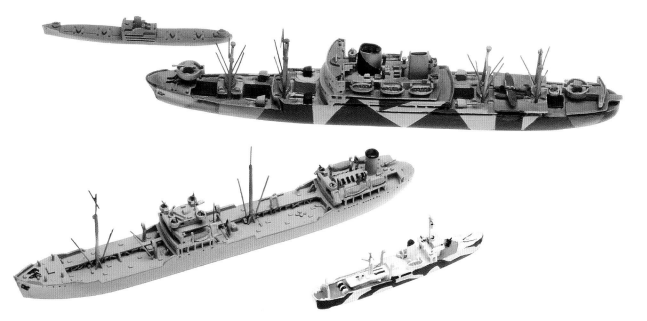

Ships oriented in approximate positions in battle, although much too close; the 1/2400 model represents *Aikoku Maru*, using forced perspective. The stern gun of *Ondina* hit the port torpedo tubes on the stern of *Hokoku Maru* while her escort steamed toward the AMCs, firing her

forward 12pdr gun. For propaganda purposes, the Indian ship was credited with firing the winning hit, but it was actually the 4in gun of *Ondina* that was responsible. Struck by three torpedoes, the empty tanker still remained afloat, and survived.

18

SPERRBRECHER SAUERLAND

Sperrbrecher (SPBs) were an important type of converted merchant ship, used widely by the Kriegsmarine for mine destruction or clearance, and little known to non-Germans although both the British and Americans used vessels for such purposes to a much lesser extent. The Italians most certainly employed mine destructor vessels, as shown by my scratch-built schooner in this

SPB 7 *Sauerland,* a used model by Förde in 1941 rig, but I converted it to 1944 specifications. Hull and superstructure are accurate, but weapons terrible with rough casting.

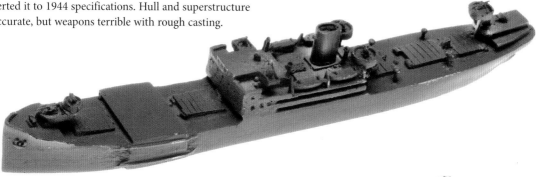

SPB stern, with barely recognisable AA; upper bandstand should be twin 37mm, while lower gun should be a quad 20mm, one of the most effective and feared weapons used by all German services for AA. Note poor quality of other structures. *Sauerland* was a much-feared escort.

Close-up of bow AA, which should represent a 10.5cm gun and a 37mm AA on upper bandstand. Förde was a small but prolific German producer of model auxiliaries, often SPBs, both ocean-going and for inland/coastal waters, the latter not made by other model producers. Many SPBs were very active in WWII.

book, although by the time depicted it might have been in German service.

The German SPBs or *Spbr* (also used in WWI), used against magnetic, pressure, acoustic or other influence mines, operated in addition to regular minesweepers carrying out traditional wire sweeps. It should be noted that many ships carried anti-mine devices on their bows, such as para-vanes for moored mines, or acoustic hammers, which can be seen in a number of ship models. SPBs cleared mines by sailing in mined waters and detonating them, hoping that their construction would offer some protection from sinking too quickly. Like many warships, SPBs were multi-functional. Besides mine destruction/detonation, they served additionally as escorts for convoys, surface warships and U-boats, and were thus

heavily armed, especially later in the war. Those running the important north-south coastal convoy routes were subject to both surface attack from small ships, especially MTBs/MGBs, and aerial assault, notably from heavily-armed Beaufighters and Mosquitoes with devastating concentrations of nose-mounted 20mm cannon and machine guns, as well as rockets, bombs and torpedoes; and single-engined fighter bombers. Period photographs of ships under such attack show them surrounded by flames and smoke. While light AA gun positions of both sides faced suppression by aerial attack (usually by gunfire or rockets), the difference in British and German AA gun protection might reflect the lethality of their respective opponents' airborne weaponry. British naval and merchant ships both had little or no

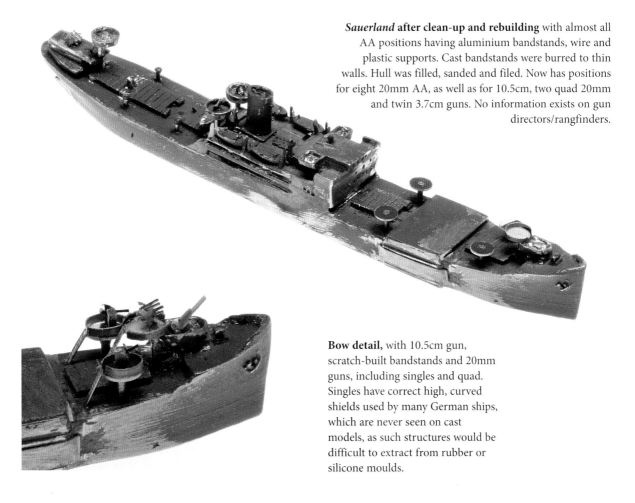

Sauerland **after clean-up and rebuilding** with almost all AA positions having aluminium bandstands, wire and plastic supports. Cast bandstands were burred to thin walls. Hull was filled, sanded and filed. Now has positions for eight 20mm AA, as well as for 10.5cm, two quad 20mm and twin 3.7cm guns. No information exists on gun directors/rangfinders.

Bow detail, with 10.5cm gun, scratch-built bandstands and 20mm guns, including singles and quad. Singles have correct high, curved shields used by many German ships, which are never seen on cast models, as such structures would be difficult to extract from rubber or silicone moulds.

shielding on their light AA. For machine guns, some single or twin Lewis guns had a slightly curved shield almost the height of the operator. Single Oerlikons had at most a small, straight plate extending from thigh to chest height, while twin 20mm had an armoured box for the gunner. In contrast, most single 20mm on German *R-boote*, trawlers, whalers, *Sperrbrecher* and other merchant vessels were furnished with a large, rounded shield that extended from the feet to above the heads of the gun crew and were large enough to shelter them all.

SPB *Sauerland* after rebuild, with mainmast of bamboo, wire and plastic, foremast with cruciform yards as seen on German destroyers, and all the weapons emplaced. Now all single 20mm AA have correct high, curved shields. The red material is recycled plastic sheet. Note that the guns, in their elevated positions on posts offering good fields of fire, are pointed in all directions, to give a sense of realism to the model. *Sauerland* was one of about 117 conversions to SPBs. Almost every *Sperrbrecher* carried one of four types of *VES-Anlagen* or electro-magnets; these generated large magnetic fields to explode magnetic mines safely at a distance. The most numerous type had the wire cables wound around the forward part of the hull, at right angles to the ship's axis (*Rundwicklung*). This area is shown on models by ribbing on the hull sides and a flat platform on the deck, often painted to resemble the wood plank covering. Photo-etched Argos crew have had to be glued on, and the model painted. Model at 12.5cm overall length reflects large size of this SPB. Most of my used Förde models were acquired through collector John Olsen, as this producer's models are not easily available in the marketplace.

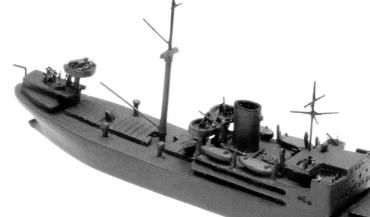

Finished rebuild of SPB *Sauerland*, with fifty-seven Argos photo-etched crew, some climbing ladders. The *VES-Anlagen* or electromagnetic wire mechanism for exploding mines is shown painted to resemble a wooden deck. This rebuild took parts of fifty-one days, a very satisfying effort to portray an important type of German warship.

19

AIRCRAFT, ALLIED AND AXIS

Taranto, Pearl Harbor and Midway clearly demonstrate the critical role played by aircraft in WWII. All aspects of the naval war depended on aircraft: protecting vessels from enemy air attack, ship strikes/bombing enemy vessels, supporting amphibious landings, convoy protection, anti-submarine and anti-ship patrols, spotting for naval gunfire, reconnaissance, minesweeping and lifeguard/air-sea rescue. Any naval ship model collection would be incomplete without aircraft models, many of which can be converted or enhanced. While 1/1200 and 1/1250 aircraft are small, and often difficult to work on, they also make ship models come alive, especially if they are accurate and carefully painted, such as those of Thomas Schroeder.

Just how effective were aircraft as anti-ship weapons and what were the most successful tactics? For both sides, combined tactics were most effective: high-level bombers, dive-bombers and torpedo bombers; the latter two categories in particular usually operated in concert. Early in the Atlantic war, German FW 200 Condors were successful with level bombing against Allied convoys, when the individual merchant ships were poorly armed with AA weapons and had little freedom to manoeuvre. German Ju 87 Stuka dive bombers were deadly when there was no air opposition; they sank the British AA ship *Foylebank* in port before she could bring many guns to bear, and were equally effective in the Mediterranean. Combined attacks by He 111s and Ju 88s, acting as either bombers or torpedo bombers, sank many Allied ships in Arctic and Mediterranean convoys. Ju 87s were the most effective German anti-ship weapon. Similarly, the Japanese 'Val', seemingly an equally antiquated dive-bomber with fixed landing gear, sank more Allied tonnage than any other of their aircraft. Long-range 'Nells' and 'Bettys' were the Japanese counterparts of He 111s

US Army Air Force, Marine and Navy aircraft: Cap Aero P38, an aircraft that was especially useful with its long-range capability; B25 converted to B25H with 75mm nose cannon for strafing and the Neptun B25 converted to Marine PBJ served in the Pacific war. The Neptun TBM, F6F and Dauntless were among the most important of US carrier aircraft; the TBM and F6F also served on British carriers and escort carriers. Catalinas served as long-range patrol bombers, as did the late-war Privateer, converted from a B24.

Neptun 'Emily', 'Mavis' and 'Jake', the Japanese four-engined flying boats being among the best of the Pacific War in terms of their long range but vulnerable to Allied aircraft guns due to inadequate protection of fuel tanks. The 'Jake' was a widely-used shipboard craft, as well as land-based. The 'Emily' model is a factory paint, while I cleaned up, painted and decaled the others.

Catalina PBY variants: Fleetline with retracted floats, Ensign waterline as PBY6A with radome, Neptun as MAD Cat with tail magnetometer and underwing rockets, Neptun Black Cat with Yagi radar antenna under wings and nose twin 20mm. These undertook patrol duties, anti-submarine patrols, even missions as torpedo bombers, as well as search and rescue or lifesaving, vital in helping maintain the morale of downed aviators.

Neptun Mariner and Kingfisher, showing the range in size of US Navy seaplanes and floatplanes. While there were American four-engine aircraft, the Catalina and the Mariner were the most active, as was the Kingfisher for shipboard duties, being launched via catapult. Both have been detailed and enhanced, with wire machine guns glued onto all gun turrets of the PBM. Neptun aircraft are usually accurate, except when moulds wear.

and Ju 88s, and deadly in their roles as bombers and torpedo planes, with the 'Betty' serving in the late war as an *Ohka* rocket bomb carrier. Though easy to shoot down due to their lack of armour, self-sealing fuel tanks and inadequate defensive armament, all Japanese aircraft nevertheless performed well.

When America entered the war, her naval aircraft could not be regarded as the equal of the Axis, although the Dauntless dive bomber essentially won the battle of Midway and continued as an excellent dive bomber for Navy and Marine pilots. Some thought it was better than the Helldiver, its successor. When the Avenger replaced the Devastator, the Navy gained a good torpedo bomber and glide bomber, also used well

Cap Aero B24, on photo of Coastal Command prototype, portions to be removed marked in black. Charred piece of Sculpy polymer was used as jig to solder the dorsal radar antenna. Photo also shows ventral pack of four 20mm cannon, also on converted model to right, along with dorsal,

nose and underwing radar antenna, latter called Yagi after Japanese inventor. Besides the ventral gun pack, the tail retains twin rear 0.50 calibre machine guns; 2.7cm wingspan. Shot with macro lens and studio strobe, thus good resolution.

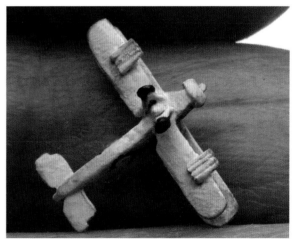

Ventral views of Swordfish and 'Betty' carrying *Ohka* rocket plane, showing enhanced British 'Stringbag' with radar and underwing rocket launchers. A Neptun 'Betty' bomber was converted to carry a scratch-built *Ohka* rocket suicide plane (0.51cm wing span). These were hard to control due to the speed of rocket propulsion.

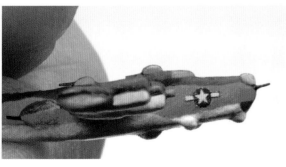

Detail of Privateer, after second rebuild, when I added ventral bulges for radar and other sensors carried by these heavily-armed late-war patrol bombers which, along with other Liberators, shot down 324 Japanese aircraft.

Japanese sea and land planes, of which 'Mavis' and 'Emily' were widely used for long-range flights; 'Betty' and 'Nell' were the most commonly used bombers, with 'Betty' converted to carry *Ohka* rocket bombs. The Zero was one of the best, often used as a fighter/escort.

German floatplanes, seaplanes and land-based aircraft, used in naval role, from various producers: He 115, BV 138, Condor, Arado 196, Ju 87, Ju 88 and He 111, latter two as torpedo bombers. The Ju 87 was a potent dive-bomber, even in 1943.

British land and sea planes used in naval roles: Coastal Command Liberator I, effective long-range patrol bomber, two variants of Sunderland (grey one converted to Mk V, with underwing radar pods, enhanced MG/cannon), Swordfish, and Beaufighters converted to 'Torbeaus', and Mosquito with 57mm nose cannon, as the 'Tsetse' version.

Delphin and HDS BV138 'Flying Clogs', both cleaned up and enhanced, with machine guns and cannon, or converted into a minesweeper, with a Dural ring for magnetic mines. Workhorses of Luftwaffe maritime operations, their wingspans are 2.13cm.

Marine PBJ and Air Force B25H, former with nose radar and twin 0.50 calibre machine guns in tail, while B25H has 0.50 calibre gun in nose, on fuselage sides and 75mm cannon on underside of nose. PBJ-1H also had 75mm.

Frontal view of above planes, with nose machine guns and 75mm cannon, seen as hole in nose. Marine PBJ has nose radar, blanked off dorsal turret and underwing rockets.

Beaufighters as 'Torbeaus', either torpedo bombers or fighters equipped with nose thimble radar, quad 20mm and underwing rockets, used to suppress German flak.

Cap Aero Mosquito as 'Tsetse', with nose 57mm cannon, underwing fuel tanks and camouflage. The nose cannon was used late in the Atlantic war to sink U-boats. This versatile and fast wooden aircraft served in multiple roles. Wingspan 1.45cm.

Close-up of Cap Aero German Ju 88 and He 111, both cleaned up and enhanced, carrying two torpedoes each and often used against Allied convoys to Russia. Wingspans are 1.50cm to 1.87cm. The Ju 88 also served as a heavy fighter when not loaded with torpedoes.

by the British on their carriers, along with the other Lend-Lease aircraft, Martlet/F4F, F6F and the Corsair. The most remarkable Royal Navy aircraft, the Swordfish, a large, slow biplane, served successfully as a torpedo bomber, as well as in A/S duties, due to its ability to take off from escort carriers and MAC ships with their short flight decks. The Beaufighter, adapted to either torpedo bomber or flak suppressor in the form of the 'Torbeau', was among the best British anti-ship strike aircraft, along with the Mosquito, some of which were armed with a Mollins 57mm nose gun,

H & R VS Neptun 'Val', the latter cleaned up, with separate Al landing gear/spats glued into slots in forward edge of wing, resulting in more correct configuration, 1.17cm wingspan.

which could sink a U-boat. These twin-engined British aircraft with a nose armament of four machine-guns and four 20mm, could put out a devastating weight of fire. The B25H carried a 75mm cannon in the nose, along with machine-guns. American B25s and A20s in the Pacific war, with as many as ten forward-firing 0.50 calibre machine guns, were equally deadly against Japanese land and naval targets. Combined with skip-bombing, this type of attack destroyed many Japanese convoys. Many British and American aircraft were up-armed with under-wing rockets, greatly increasing their firepower without adding too much weight.

The aircraft in this chapter represent the most often used in the naval war. While small and difficult to model well, they are worth the effort due to the paramount role aircraft played in WWII. Often, battles were decided without any ships coming into contact, only the aircraft that they carried.

Conversion of B24, plus finished Privateers. Left-hand image shows unknown make of B24 converted with plastic tail and metal/plastic turrets into Privateer. Right-hand image shows finished conversion, with wire machine guns and three-tone colour scheme, along with slightly smaller

resin Privateer by Vota Plane (made by Brian Vota). Wingspans 2.85cm and 2.60cm respectively. RKL Privateer, shown on p.115, converted second time to include ventral sensors and radar.

20

CONVERSION FOR WAR

The most important and numerous of ship types converted for war during WWII included armed merchant cruisers (AMCs) or *Hilfskreuzer* (HCs/HSKs); the similar ocean boarding vessels (OBVs); mine destructor/clearance/countermeasures vessels or *Sperrbrecher*; and the largest class, trawlers and whalers, including other similar fishing vessels, particularly those used by the Japanese as picket or guard boats. While strategically not important, though surprisingly numerous, especially in Japanese service, I added sailing vessels, some armed, to this chapter, because they caught my imagination. For the Germany Navy, SPBs and trawlers, in all their

manifestations, were probably the most active of their surface ships, while trawlers of the Commonwealth navies were almost as heavily engaged. These sturdy vessels derived from the fishing industry were vital for anti-submarine, minesweeping, escort and flak duties. Besides the ship classes above, CAM ships, MAC ships, Fighter Catapult Ships (FCS), AA ships and gunboats of various types and origins, Q-ships, watch/guard ships and picket boats are also germane, as these were also usually converted from merchant ships, though some, such as British AA, FCSs and MAC ships, often required extensive rebuilds. Certainly rebuilds or *umbau*, often

Allied and Axis ships converted for war from merchant ships: Albatross 120 AMC *Cilicia*, with eight partially-shielded 6in guns, nine assorted AA, 14.3cm overall length; Förde SPB *Sauerland*, extensively rebuilt, one 10.5cm, two 37mm, two quad 20mm, eight single, shielded 20mm, with Argos photo-etched crew, 12.5cm overall length; cleaned

up/detailed Argonaut British trawler *Bay* 4.1cm overall length; JB 1b T German trawler, 4.7cm overall length; two armed, modified caiques as used in the Aegean, by both the British and the Germans. Facing page shows more conversions for war, some stock, others cleaned up or heavily re-worked.

Warrior K7 British CAM ship *Empire Day* before correction,
(Len Jordan resin 1/1200 model completed and painted by
Robert Slough), 11.6cm overall length; Hai 314 British MAC
ship *Empire MacAlpine*, 10.7cm overall length with
Figurehead Swordfish; Helge Fischer HF36 German floating
AA battery *Medusa*, 8.4cm overall length; Argonaut 192
British AA ship *Tynwald*, 8.0cm overall length; Santa Rosa
SR15a British auxiliary paddlewheel AA ship *Aristocrat*
(resin, 1/1200), 5.4 cm overall length; Figurehead CB44
British LCG(L3), 4.5cm overall length; Neptun N1389e US

LCS (L), 3.95cm overall length;
Trident T1231 British LCG (M2), 3.8cm overall length; Förde
216 German Schiff 13/Saturn, a Q-ship trawler, 4.55cm
overall length. *Back row:* Hai 50 British LCF, 4.5cm overall
length; Förde 157 German SAT Ost, 4.1 cm overall length;
Trident 1148 German AFP C2, 3.9cm overall length;
Rhenania RSKM29 German AF 42, 3.8cm overall length;
Rhenania RSKM 18D German *MAL 13-36 Typ lc*,2.8cm
overall length; Rhenania RSKM 22 German *Siebel* ferry *SF 40*,
1.95cm overall length; Risawoleska Ri 64b German *Marsk
Stig*, an armed Danish ferry, 5.8cm overall length.

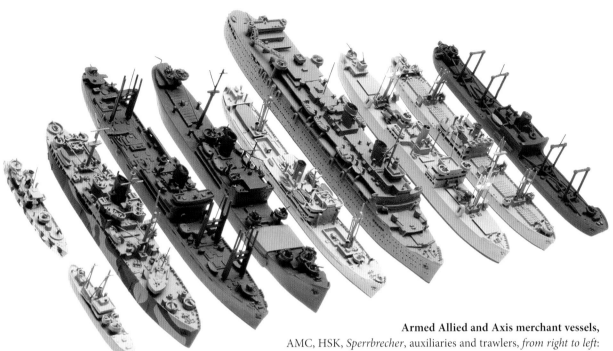

Armed Allied and Axis merchant vessels,
AMC, HSK, *Sperrbrecher*, auxiliaries and trawlers, *from right to left*:
Trident *Canberra Maru*; Neptun 'Liberty' ship; Santa Rosa resin *Fort
Halket* with two Hudson aircraft as deck cargo; Albatros AMC *Queen of
Bermuda*; Neptun HSK *Michel*; Förde SPB *Sauerland*; Neptun *Kimikawa
Maru* seaplane carrier; Sea Vee AGP *Acontius* PT boat tender; *JB*
camouflaged *Vorpostenboote*; Oceanic trawler *Coll*.

**German vs British
trawlers/whalers,** with left-
hand column of German
Figurehead CG41 whaler; Sextant
Star 23 whaler; Argonaut *Strymon*;
Mercator M052; *JB*16t; Neptun N1085 KUJ
1-25; right-hand column of British Figurehead
CB42; Clydeside *Isles* trawler; Argonaut 1235 *Bern*;
Argonaut *Basset*; Navwar (?) *M46*; Figurehead CB41
whaler. 2.7cm to 4.8cm overall length.

British AMCs and OBVs, *right, from top to bottom*: Albatros *Carnarvon Castle, Alcantara,* Len Jordan resin *Ranpura,* Albatros *Queen of Bermuda,* Colonia *Jervis Bay,* Albatros *Cilicia*, Argonaut OBV *Cavina* and Albatros OBV *Cavina*, 11.3 to 16.8cm overall length. Both the ocean boarding vessels are now enhanced and finished, with all AA installed. The *Ranpura* was a kit, very well cast, and the *Jervis Bay* was extensively reworked and corrected. *Queen of Bermuda* was one of two British AMCs that carried floatplanes, in this case American Kingfishers. British AMCs were converted from liners, whereas German HSKs were usually former fruit carriers, smaller and faster.

Argonaut 1231 (11.3 cm OA) vs Albatros 103 (11.4cm OA) *Cavina* OBV to show differences in accuracy of modelling and casting quality, evident by missing portions of boat deck, many other poorly-cast features and peeling paint on Argonaut model and inclusion of all primary and secondary weapons by Albatros, but only posts for some by Argonaut. Cargo booms are cast in one, metal wires in the other; both have bow paravane A-frames. Below, the Argonaut is being restored and enhanced; the upper photograph shows both models after enhancements and repainting. It is always instructive to see how different manufacturers cover the same subject.

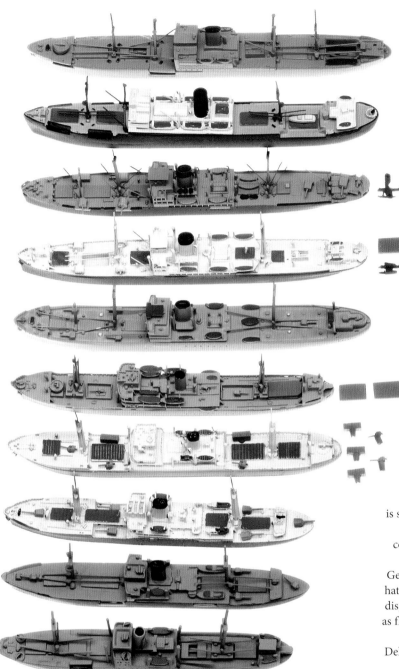

Models of German auxiliary cruisers by Delphin, Sextant, Rhenania, Neptun and Hansa: as with any model ship manufacturers, there are a great number of differences in the casting and accuracy of the models. This image gives an idea of the range in sizes and armament concealment devices used on the model, subject to how well the prototype was followed. *Komoran* (top), by Delphin, is largest, at 13.3cm overall length; Hansa's *Komet* is smallest at 9.1cm overall length, which has been modified by the author to show concealed forward port gun, revealed when deck/bulwark was opened. The better German producers often supplied removable hatch covers, turrets and camouflaged turrets disguised as crates or bundles of rope, as well as floatplanes. Models are *Kormoran, Atlantis, Widder, Orion, Michel, Stier,* Neptun *Thor,* Delphin *Thor* and *Komet. Kormoran* sank the Australian light cruiser *Sydney.*

repeated a number of times in German ships such as SPBs and trawlers, were mainly to increase their AA armament and mine-clearance abilities. SPBs required complex hull and internal alterations for their electromagnetic anti-mine devices. As for gunboats, some were existing naval ships adapted to other functions, such as landing craft which the British converted to AA (LCF) or gunboats (LCG), the American conversion of subchasers to PGM/small gunboats or of landing craft infantry to LCI (G) or LCS(L), with various armament fits of guns, mortars and rockets. The Kriegsmarine used up-armed landing craft as small SPBs and gunboats, such as *Artilleriefaehrpraehme* (AFs),

Comparison of Delphin and Neptun *Thor*, 9.7cm and 10.0cm overall length respectively. Primary distinction is modelling two of the main guns behind bulwarks by Delphin, which follows the prototype. While the Neptun version has much more detail it is also in some places less accurate. Second hull opening on Delphin shows torpedo tubes, often carried by Axis AMCs.

Marine-Artillerie-Leichter (MALs) and *Siebel* ferries. But others within this classification had merchant ship origins, either coasters converted into gunboats known as *Schwere-Artillerie-Traeger* (SATs) by the Germans, or dredgers into similar gunboats by the Soviets, the latter ironically also of German origin. While some of the ship classes converted for war numbered in the thousands, such as trawlers, almost all the vessel types discussed in this book are poorly represented among ship models. The exception are SPBs and trawlers/whalers, the former made almost exclusively by German manufacturers, although most are now out of production and only available on the second-hand market. In fact, the now defunct German maker Förde, which only sold directly to collectors, is alone responsible for most of the German *Sperrbrecher* and many of their trawlers; this manufacturer usually produced model ships with good lines but was often very poor on details, so that extensive rebuilds are necessary. The next most numerous types of merchant ships converted for war are AMCs or HSKs, which were active early in WWII.

Axis AMCs Hai *Hokoku Maru*, Degen resin *Citti di Tunisia* and WI resin Italian *Lero*, which is 6.6cm overall length.

Armed trawlers, whalers, drifters, luggers and similar ships derived from fishing vessels comprised the largest category of any naval ships

Close-up showing details of *Hokoku Maru* and Neptun *Orion*, showing 'Jake' carried on aft deck of the former, although this should be a 'Pete', and an Arado 196 floatplane with folded wings in the forward hold of *Orion*; thus illustrating two different ways in which these ships carried their aircraft.

Neptun 1394 'Liberty' ship vs Neptun 1023 HSK *Stier*:
US *Stephen Hopkins* engaged the German raider *Stier* and the supply ship *Tannefels* in the South Atlantic when the ships emerged out of fog at close range; outgunned, this gallant cargo vessel was sunk but fought so hard with her 4in stern gun and AA that the Germans thought she was an AMC. *Stier* was so badly hit that she was later scuttled. The Neptun version is of a later 'Liberty' ship, *Jeremiah O'Brien* (now a museum ship). The model has a bow 3in and a stern 4in gun, plus eight 20mm, in contrast to only one 4in, two 37mm and six machine guns for the actual *Stephen Hopkins*; the model is 10.6cm overall length. Captain Gerlach of the *Stier* thought the enemy ship had a 6in at the stern, plus

four 4.7in at the stern and four more amidships. Early in the battle, a 15cm shell hit the *Hopkins'* starboard boiler, so her speed dropped to one knot. Despite most of the stern gun's teenaged crew of Naval Armed Guard and Merchant Marine replacements being mortally wounded, the American 4in hit the HSK fifteen times, in about a quarter of an hour period, while the *Stier*'s main-battery of six guns hit the 'Liberty' ship with fifty to sixty salvos. The *Stier* model displays three shielded guns, one unshielded gun on the poop deck and two removable crates representing the balance of the main guns, although only a few 20mm of her large AA fit is shown. *Stier*'s turreted guns are trainable and removable.

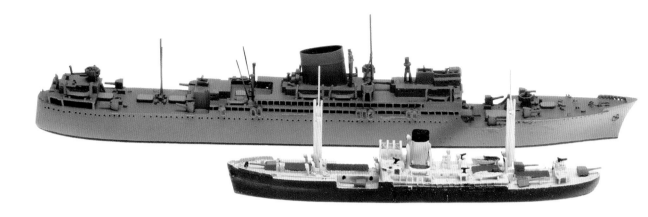

Albatros-K 121 *Carnarvon Castle* vs Neptun *Thor*
invoking images of David and Goliath, respectively 16.8cm
and 9.7cm overall length. The larger British AMC and *Thor*,
a former fruit ship, fought one another in 1940; the former
fired over 600 rounds of 6in with no hits while the
Hilfkreuzer struck the *Carnarvon Castle* twenty-seven times
out of 593 shots. That same year, *Thor* damaged the large
AMC *Alcantara* and in 1941, sunk the *Voltaire*, another

British AMC. Her opponents were liners and matched or
exceeded her main gun batteries with eight of their own,
although the British guns were antiquated, with less
elevation and thus range, and less well-directed, as well as
having less practised gun crews. The image below shows the
Albatros *Alcantara* with Delphin D33 *Thor*. Note that both
British AMCs mount radar on towers forward of their
funnels.

in WWII. Excluding Commonwealth units, other
Allied navies and reverse Lend-Lease, which
included twenty to twenty-four trawlers and two
whalers for the US Navy, the British alone used
1,513 such ships. This probably included similar

ships from Norway, the Netherlands, France and
Belgium which escaped the German occupation of
the Continent in 1940 and fled to British ports,
being then taken over and manned by them subsequently.

21

CONVOY RESCUE SHIPS

onvoy instructions dictated that the last ship in a column acted as a rescue ship, but that ship often could not or would not fulfill its duty. If a ship was empty and in ballast, the freeboard might be too high to effect a rescue. If a merchant ship, it might be too dangerous for the ship to stop and risk being torpedoed. Devastating losses in cargo vessels and tankers and their irreplaceable crews from a finite pool of qualified merchant marine sailors led in 1940 to the C-in-C of Western Approaches to recommend the establishment of specific convoy rescue ships, of which none were then available. Ships from the British coastal trade were selected, as they had a lower

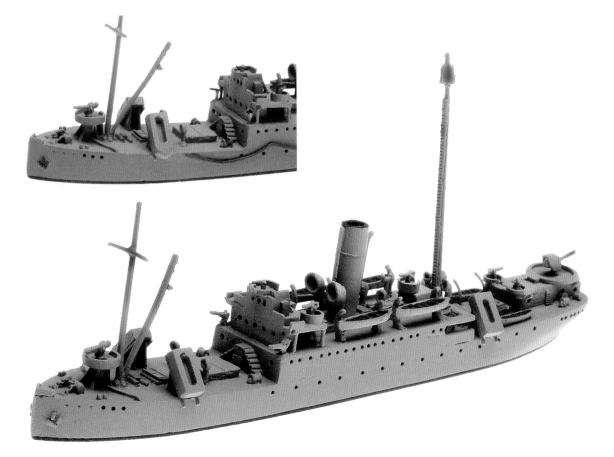

Spider Navy SN 2-10 convoy rescue ship *Goodwin* as received, a gift from son Patrick; a well-cast model, as expected from this well-regarded German producer. 6.6cm overall length. Note the very large twin guns forward of bridge, and square-ended life rafts. In inset photo of the forward portion of the model as corrected and enhanced, these have been replaced by appropriate machine guns and pointed life rafts, as well as lifeline attached to hull.

freeboard and greater capacity to house survivors than other ships of their size, usually around 250ft (76m) overall length and 1,500 tons gross. Twenty-four such coasters were modified into convoy rescue ships, as well as later five 'Castle' class corvettes, with berthing and medical facilities, usually decent AA armament for the coasters, lifeboats more suited for the open sea and, perhaps most importantly, the installation of a H/F antenna, usually only carried by convoy escorts. An additional HF/DF allowed the convoy to more easily triangulate very high frequency (VHF) radio transmissions from U-boats, enabling convoy escorts to locate them more easily. The Special Service Vessel HMS *Fidelity* was both an escort and convoy rescue ship, heavily armed and carrying an MTB and two Kingfisher floatplanes. Convoy rescue ships and their crews were well-respected and well-protected by convoy escorts. Over 4,000 survivors were rescued, including aircrew, as these ships also acted as plane guards for MAC ships. Not only were the lives of vital personnel saved, but these vessels were also a great boost to the morale of those serving on convoys.

Plan view of *Goodwin*, after corrections and enhancements: life rafts are now pointed, instead of square; oversize twin machine guns forward of bridge replaced with smaller machine guns, meant to represent twin Lewis guns. The port lifeboats are now swung outboard, ready for lowering, and one is now a motorised cutter, for more maneuverability, desirable when rescuing survivors. Lifelines are now slung along the hull, a feature of all convoy rescue ships. Image below shows my attempt to replace the solid, cast HF/DF antenna on mainmast with a more accurate wire version. This proved not to be possible, for even with the plastic jigs I made I could not bend the wire to the HF/DF shape.

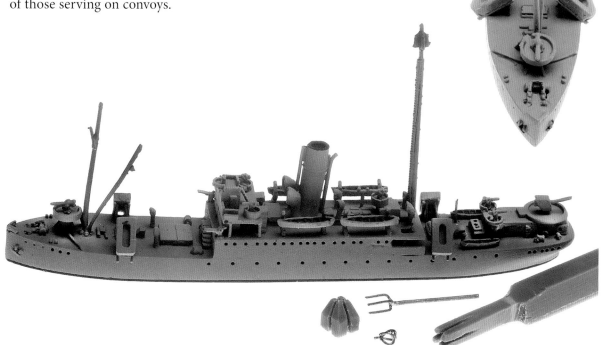

There is only one available convoy rescue ship model, HMS *Goodwin*, produced by the well-known maker Spider Navy. Well-mastered and cast, there are nevertheless problems with this model: all the life rafts are square, without the pointed noses as seen in almost all convoy rescue ships, except in one clear but unidentified image of *Gothland*, and the twin machine guns forward of the bridge are oversize, larger than the 20mm. Almost all such ships carried some of their lifeboats swung outboard, ready for use. Less problematical is the lack of lifelines slung along the hull sides, a permanent feature of rescue ships. Some of these features might have been difficult to execute in a cast model. Through the help of my German friend and fellow modeller Niels Neelsen, I was able to obtain plans for *Goodwin*, so that I could correct the oversize machine guns, which were probably twin Lewis guns. The other modifications could be done by looking at images in Hague's *Convoy Rescue Ships*. I tried to replace the HF/DF antenna with a more accurate wire one, but was not able to do so, even with special plastic jigs, due to the complexity and tiny size of this vital equipment. Very few have been able to do this, except the master German modeller Peter Ohm and the model producer Sea Vee. The *Goodwin* is nevertheless still a vital and welcome model for anyone interested in WWII convoys.

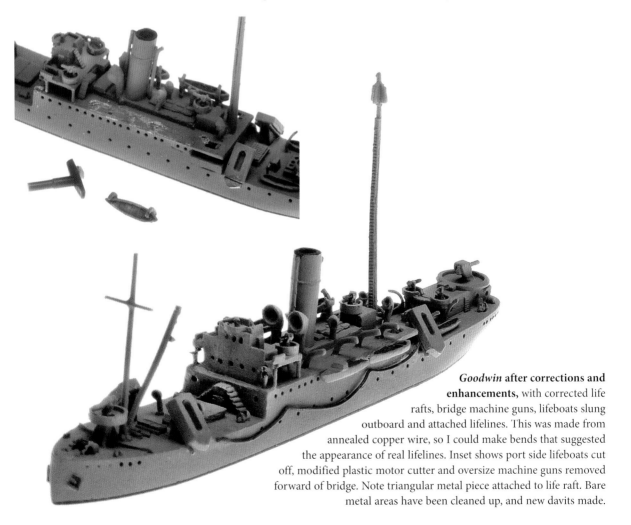

Goodwin **after corrections and enhancements,** with corrected life rafts, bridge machine guns, lifeboats slung outboard and attached lifelines. This was made from annealed copper wire, so I could make bends that suggested the appearance of real lifelines. Inset shows port side lifeboats cut off, modified plastic motor cutter and oversize machine guns removed forward of bridge. Note triangular metal piece attached to life raft. Bare metal areas have been cleaned up, and new davits made.

22

FCS/AA SHIP *SPRINGBANK*

Given that small-scale naval ship models are often produced in short runs, and not then re-cast when the rubber or silicone moulds deteriorate, it is often the case that the wish to own a particular ship model does not match availability. Such was the case with the auxiliary anti-aircraft ship/fighter catapult ship (FCS) *Springbank*, meaning I instead bought a rather inaccurate handmade wooden example, stripped it down to the hull, corrected that, and then rebuilt the entire model. Then subsequently a metal model

of *Alynbank*, a near sister ship, became available.

However, as shown on this page, with this commercial model, though well made, its secondary and tertiary AA armament was inaccurate. Even though this rebuild took 88 hours, spread out over the course of some 59 evenings, I do not regret it and, as with each of these complex projects, I improved my model-making skills, and ended up with a fine record and a memorial to those who served on these ships. At the heart of small-scale modelmaking is how to reduce a

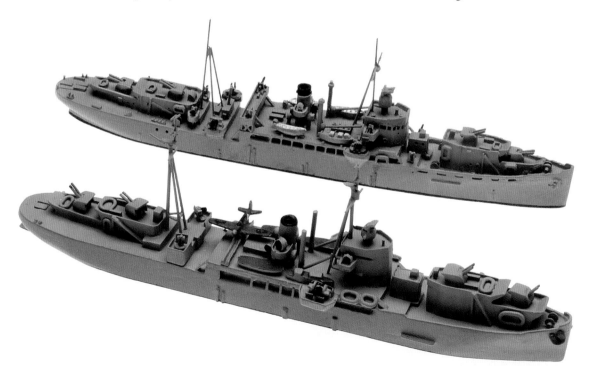

Comparison of author's *Springbank* vs Argonaut *Alynbank*, a near sister ship, which should be identical except lacking a catapult and fighter. The latter is a nice, used model with some repair, but entirely incorrect as to AA. *Alynbank* has two extra quad pom-poms, eight 20mm

(note: not mentioned in references) and the quad 0.50 machine guns were in the wrong position. She should be equipped like *Springbank* in terms of AA guns and their dispositions. I did not own the *Alynbank* model until after I had built the *Springbank*, which is 10.7cm overall length

Comparison of Miles S. Vaughn hardwood *Springbank*, partially enhanced balsa Hartings *Springbank* and author's old balsa hull from late 1940s-early 1950s: note the variety of 4in turrets on first two *Springbank*s, some scratch-built, others from various manufacturers' castings, as well as incorrect positions of multiple pom-poms on the Vaughn model. After trying to correct the Hartings model with a corrected bow, I decided to strip the Vaughn model completely and rebuild, and to strip the Hartings model as it was too poor to keep. I eventually used my old balsa/styrene hull (9.3cm overall length) to rebuild as the *Prince Robert*.

Vaughn was a well-known US dealer of used models, often sold to wargamers; he had lived in Japan before the war, and carried some unusual models. Hartings was a prolific builder of balsa wood naval ship models, that were then sold by Vaughn. Though once described as the Michaelangelo of ship model builders, one can see from these examples that this label is not really warranted. Still, it is important for collectors and ship modellers to study first-hand the work of others before judging their merits, although if one does not retain such models, it can be an expensive way to learn.

complex structure, like the quad 2pdr pom-pom, to a 1/1200 or 1/1250 scale size, yet retain the accuracy and characteristic appearance of such an item. In a sense, working in this scale is more like creating an illusion, rather than actual total fidelity. For the experienced collector/modeller, one can tell at a glance whether a ship or aircraft model has captured the appearance of the original. The ability to do this hinges on modelling skills, as well as having thoroughly studied enough reference material. A well-stocked library or a careful Internet search is just as useful and imp-

ortant as a workbench with the appropriate tools.

The *Springbank* served a dual purpose, having a catapult with which she could launch one of two Fulmar fighters to repel aircraft threatening the convoys she protected, and additionally a relatively powerful AA armament. Many of these auxiliary AA ships were sunk but, along with older cruisers converted to AA ships and purpose-built AA cruisers like the *Dido* class, they played an important role in protecting convoys from aerial attack, especially in the Mediterranean and in the Arctic. The vulnerability of converted

HMS *Springbank* by Miles S. Vaughn, made in
the 1960s–70s of hardwood, shown before it was
stripped down to hull and partial superstructure,
prior to hull and bow being rebuilt. The turrets
were metal castings from various ship models, as
well as the quad pom-poms, but there were no
quad machine guns nor masts.

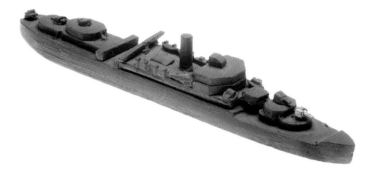

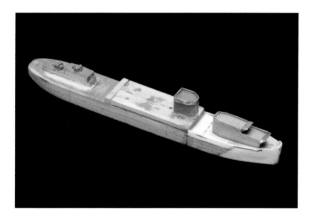

Partially stripped *Springbank,* with front of hull sandwiched with
plastic sheet, bulwarks fitted, and a solid bridge structure of correct
configuration installed, made from a large piece of plastic sprue. Some
time after the model was finished, I realised that all models of
Springbank and *Alynbank* had incorrect bridges, as they were undercut
aft, and not solid as I and others had made them. Perhaps we had
all used the same sketch in *All the World's Fighting Ships* as a
reference; this small sketch did not show the extension of
the upper bridge deck, giving an undercut look to the
bridge structure. At this point of the build, I still
retained the aft gun-deck and cast turrets.

Stripped and rebuilding *Springbank,* with forward gun-
decks of plastic sprue and aluminium sheet. The bridge now
has additional aluminium strip; note that it rests on a
portion of original wood superstructure. Stern still retains
Vaughn's gun-deck and turrets. Most of the wooden hull has
been sanded. Hardwood, possibly basswood, has less grain
than balsa, and thus results in a smoother finish. When
strongly glued, it is not difficult to join plastic and wood.

Close-up of forward gun-deck, made of aluminium sheet
and thick plastic sprue leftover from kits. These blast shields
or zarebas served to protect the gunners of the twin 4in AA
guns from blast or concussion, as the turrets were open and
most of the gun crew were exposed. Note that the turret is of
plastic, clad with aluminium sheet, with a grooved piece of
metal to represent the twin breeches of the guns. These
barrels are of iron binding wire which, while not possible to
taper, is slim enough to simulate the long barrels of the
actual weapons. Cyano-acrylic glue was used to glue all the
components, with cracks filled by Bondo, an automobile
filler that is long-lasting and inexpensive. After glue has
dried and bonded, everything is filed or sanded to square it
all up, resulting in the visible bare aluminium metal.

After some consideration, I decided that it would be better to replace all components so that the model was uniform in appearance and accuracy. At this stage, only the hull and the first deck of the superstructure have been retained from the original *Springbank*. A gun director and its radar have been installed on the bridge, as well all the gun-decks and main armament. The red marks are to help me accurately install turrets and other structures, but are not definitive.

Close-up of gun-decks, turrets and bridge, before I glued them in place. Using permanent marker ink like the red can cause problems with water-based paints, when the alcohol-based ink bleeds through. The red on the plastic is the outer coating of the scrap sheet I used, and not red marker pen. This model was easier to make than the *Prince Robert*, as it is more spacious, with less crowding of the superstructure and deck fittings. When I am constructing models, especially complex ones, I try to photographically document each step, usually in the office photo studio, and this entails packing them carefully for the journey from home and back again afterwards.

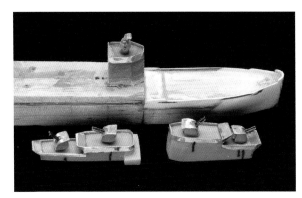

Close-up of *Springbank* build, with most of the main components made and many glued in place, including the aluminium funnel and its attached searchlight platforms, the bridge, complete with wing, the starboard quad pom-pom, while the port sponson and AA mount are loose. These quad weapons require at least sixteen pieces for the guns, more for the aluminium base and sponson. Note the metal catapult and, aft of it, the two quad 0.50 calibre water-cooled machine guns, which were relatively useless in their AA role. The bare metal aircraft is a much cleaned-up Cap Aero Fulmar. The tripod legs of the foremast can be seen.

AA ships lay in their origins as merchant ships, lacking the armour and sufficient watertight bulkheads to withstand bomb, torpedo or gunnery hits, and their much slower speeds. British AMCs did try to compensate for their weaker hulls by loading empty, sealed oil drums to increase buoyancy. German *Sperrbrecher* had more elaborate schemes to counter mine explosions, loading layered materials to absorb shock as well as empty oil drums.

On the model of *Springbank,* only the Fulmar fighter was not scratch-built. All the building materials were what every modeller accumulates over time, so there was relatively little cost for these, although tools and a library take both time and expense to bring together. The most expensive element is time, particularly if one were to think of it in terms of an hourly rate. But to me, it is the challenge of making the best model I can, given the time I can or want to allot to that task. When a collector sees the high price for a well-built, converted, enhanced or scratch-built model, he should bear in mind the skills and the sheer amount of labour and concentration involved in

Close-up of *Springbank* build, with correction for placement of catapult, now moved forward. In this enlarged view, you can clearly see details like how the quad machine guns are made, with separate pieces of wire for the barrels, plastic for the gun mechanisms and a slightly curved aluminium shield for the gunner. In foreground are multiples of British Type 279 radar, made from thin 26-gauge copper wire. For very small items such as these, it is easier to glue larger pieces, before trimming to size, than to make them actual size first. The thicker loops of copper wire will become Carley floats, with glue/paint filling the gaps.

Close-up of forward part of ship, turrets, Carley floats, ready-use ammo boxes, ladders and winch. Aft of the deckhouse is the bridge, complete with tripod mast, yard, braces, crow's nest and radars for the gun director. Note the strake on the hull and the still empty sponsons for the quad pom-poms. Bondo has been used to fill gaps.

Close-up of stern, with more details added. Hand-carved plastic ventilators surround the funnel, the cordite-propelled catapult now has a sled of copper wire, and the mainmast is installed, with all legs set into drilled holes for strength. The stern gun-decks are similarly equipped as the forward oness, with Carley floats made of loops of wire. The joins fill with paint and are not noticeable. Note the aluminium rudder at the stern. Various discharge pipes are adhered to the hull.

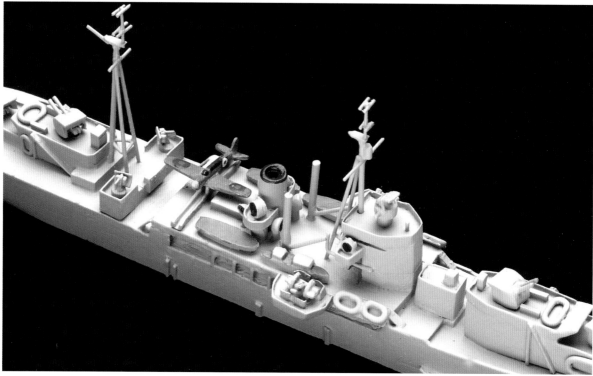

creating a complex and accurate model. Though many of the best production models are expensive, these cast metal examples are rarely as accurate as hand-built models, where metal or plastic strip and wire enable the creation of thinner, possibly stronger and more accurate features, especially gun barrels, bulwarks and masts. One of the limiting factors in building accurate models is the difficulty of holding and working tiny parts with precision. These can easily be dropped and so become lost.

If one looks at photographs of the finished but unpainted *Springbank* and the painted model, it is not easy to see that the total number of individual items that comprise a scratch-built ship model. A rough count of my painted *Springbank* in the image suggests only twenty-odd structures. But examination of the upper photo on the facing

page, depicting only the mid-portion of the model, indicates 140 individual pieces of plastic, metal sheet and rod, as well as wires of different diameters and metal types. When you remember that almost all these pieces had to be filed or cut into their shape and size, then carefully glued, you can appreciate the amount of time required for scratch-building a miniature naval ship model.

Completed *Springbank*, shown prior to (*opposite, above*) and after (*below*) painting, now with lifeboats/cutters added, as well as booms for the boats. Automotive enamel spray paint was used, then details were hand-painted. A black wash was applied to all AA barrels, as these were not painted. Fulmar has been detailed and adds colour to the otherwise drab converted merchant ship. The model still needs running lights.

Plan view comparison of author's *Springbank* vs Argonaut *Alynbank*, a metal cast model from a well-known German producer of British warship models. The *Alynbank* was a sister ship, although she was not equipped with a catapult or fighter. Her hull is finer than mine and has smaller sponsons for the quad pom-poms, but *Alynbank* has two extra quad pom-poms, eight 20mm (note: not mentioned in reference works) and the quad 0.50 calibre machine guns are in an incorrect position. She should be equipped like *Springbank* in terms of AA guns and their dispositions. *Alynbank* was sunk as a blockship at Normandy for the D-Day artificial harbours while *Springbank* was sunk by a German submarine in 1941.

23

AA SHIP *PRINCE ROBERT*

Like actual naval vessels, ship models are often rebuilt. My model of the Canadian anti-aircraft ship HMCS *Prince Robert* was one such model, based on a stripped balsa hull of a merchant ship I had made in the late 1940s or early 1950s when my late mechanical engineer brother John was teaching me how to make wooden ship models, using nothing more than a razor blade, some files and sandpaper. This hull became the basis for a 1/1250 *Prince Robert*, sister to *Prince Henry* and *Prince David*. All three were modern passenger ships built for the Canadian national railways in 1930 and converted at the start of WWII into AMCs. By 1943 *Prince Robert* had been rebuilt as an AA ship, serving as a convoy escort, while her two sister ships were converted into Infantry Landing Ships (LSIs), in preparation for their use for landings on the European continent.

With my interest in merchant ships being used as warships, it was a natural to choose *Prince Robert* as a scratch-build project, depicting her in 1943, before her final refit and re-armament. This ship had a complex superstructure and armament, plus a striking camouflage scheme, and required lots of research. When I started the build, I only

***Prince Robert* by Optatus vs my scratch-built *Prince Robert*.** Because the foam packing material stuck to the funnels and pulled off the paint when cleaned up, I had to re-spray the metal *Prince Robert* with TS 66, Tamiya's Kure grey, as well as do a clean up of the hull and taper the main guns. The Optatus model has no 20mm guns and shows differences in the bridge superstructure and other structures, like the gun director, as well as longer 4in gun barrels and soldered masts and davits. Soldering is done by a few European producers. Optatus has a more accurate Carley float platform than my model, but lacks stern depth-charge chutes (see inset). Both are 9.3cm overall length.

138

had an Argonaut *Prince Henry* AMC for reference, in addition to Darlington and McKee's *Three Princes Armed* and what information I could gather from the Internet. After completion of the model, I was able to acquire the Optatus *Prince Robert* for comparison, as shown. As usual with my model ship builds, there were no plans and only a few clear photographs were available, so it was difficult to locate accurately the positions of the six 20mm AA (this may be why the Optatus *Prince Robert* lacks these guns). Since all parts were scratch-built, this took much time and work; each quad pom-pom consisted of sixteen different minute parts. Besides the six single 20mm, this AA ship had two quad 2pdr pom-poms installed in sponsons aft, as well as ten 4in guns; a formidable armament. Darlington and McKee state that six more 20mm were added, totalling twelve, but no images seem to exist showing this configuration. The main AA guns were in mounts open at the rear, so breeches had to be made for the guns, as well as blast shields or zarebas to protect the gunners from concussion or blast.

I utilised my usual mix of materials, including wood, plastic sprue and sheet, aluminium sheet and rod, copper, brass and steel wire. Aluminium sheet from quick-print plates was cut into sheets or strips with a paper cutter and formed with thin-nosed pliers into bulwarks for the bridge as well as for the blast shields of gun decks, to near scale thicknesses. Upper deck structure was two plastic pieces, joined with aluminium reinforcement.

Of course, like all model projects, nothing proceeded smoothly: new techniques had to be tried, parts broke or were lost and building multiple parts required time-consuming serial fabrication. With delicate components like the lattice tower for radar, masts, yards and HF/DF and navigational antenna, it was easy to knock one part off while another was being fitted. In addition, where so many parts are crammed into a relatively short space of 9.3cm, mistakes in making components even slightly oversize build up, to a point where one has to rebuild in order to fit everything in its relatively correct position on the hull. Good practices like drilling holes when

Argonaut *Prince Henry* vs my old hull of balsa.
I sandwiched the wood with plastic sheet and corrected the bow and stern, the former with plastic. The metal *Prince Henry* helped me to obtain the correct basic form and dimensions of the ship, as the two were sister ships.

Bridge, gun director, and forward gun-deck of *Prince Robert,* made of plastic and aluminium sheet, lattice mast and radar of copper wire, and Type 271 radar housing of aluminium rod shaped by file. Red is Bondo filler, and permanent ink marker pen for noting position of 'B' turret.

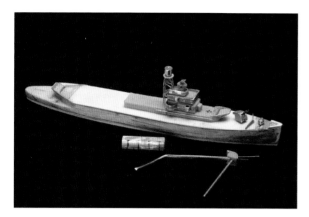

Partially-built model, with forward 4in turret; in foreground is aluminium-covered plastic sprue, marked for sawing. To right is 4in turret in progress, with grooved brass rod for the breech and mounting rod, showing how these mountings were batch made.

Close-ups of bridge and nearly completed model, showing how many individual parts had to be fabricated. The balsa hull has an aluminium strake and the anchor is recessed, a hallmark of these three sisters. Note the layers of paint and fillers on the hull, which still needs to be sanded smooth, as well as the grain of the balsa, a problem with this soft wood.

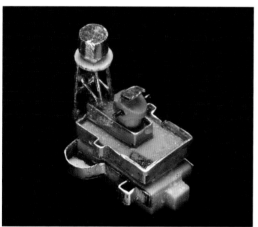

Completed *Prince Robert*, prior to final priming. Virtually every part is an individual piece, which is why this model took some 45 partial days to complete. The most complex parts are the quad pom-poms, which comprise sixteen pieces each (see inset). You can observe my preference for copper wire, which is easy to work and does not adhere to metal tweezers, which all become magnetic over time, making ferrous material hard to release when gluing delicate parts.

gluing in wires also helps to strengthen a model, as seen in the image of the ships that dropped onto the studio floor from a height of two to three feet during photography.

Painting of the deck and camouflage schemes involved much retouching, as it is almost impossible not to inadvertently paint the wrong part when space is so tight. Retouching required scraping with a sharp craft knife blade tip and repainting. Primary colours for *Prince Robert* were GHQ Sea Blue and Tamiya Flat White, both acrylics, although I had to blend other colours into the blue to achieve the correct tone as used on the actual ship.

Prince Robert **in base paint** vs partially rebuilt Hartings hull for testing paint. Since I only had small colour reproductions of paintings on which to base my base paint and camouflage colours of *Prince Robert*, my approximations may not be too accurate. The base paint was auto primer enamel from a spray can. I tested various colours on the hull of a Hartings *Prince Robert,* a wooden model which was too poor to improve further. Good b/w photos of the starboard patterns exist but not those of the port side, so that was down to guesswork.

Prince Robert **and** *Springbank,* after they had been dropped while in the photography studio. Fortunately, due to the light weight of these wooden models, damage was mostly limited to the masts, although the Fulmar fighter was knocked off *Springbank*'s catapult. The mainmast of *Springbank* broke off almost intact, while the foremast was only bent. *Prince Robert* shows mostly wooden deck but I had no reliable information as to which of the decks of *Springbank* were wooden, so all the decks were left in plain naval grey.

24

ITALIAN ARMED SCHOONER

Serendipity provides some of the most useful information for modelmaking. A photograph of two German Bf 110s overflying at least three sailing vessels in North Africa appears in Gunston's 1978 encyclopedia of WWII aircraft. Although the photograph is grainy, it does present an excellent three-quarter aerial view of a two-masted schooner, devoid of sails, with bandstands for guns fore and aft and unusual symmetrical overhanging platforms on both sides of the vessel, as well as a rather complex superstructure for a sailing vessel. Side or lateral views of any kind would never have enabled one to determine the nature of such overhangs or deck structures. Later, I chanced upon Ethell's *Luftwaffe at War 4*, which had the same photo on the cover and inside, with much better resolution, identifying the image as German aircraft flying over the harbour at Tripoli,

Libya, then in Axis hands, after crossing the Mediterranean. Many small boats were visible, about six of which were schooners. But only the schooner illustrated was visibly equipped for weapons and had the vastly altered superstructure, although the two bandstands were empty. These were probably for 37mm or 76mm guns. Based on measurements estimated from the photograph, this two-masted vessel appears to have been between 150 and 180ft (50–60m) long.

This unusual vessel is a SPB, identified as such because of the similarity to some of the structures on the German *Sperrbrecher* 195, the ex-*Santa Rita*; indeed it may have been the same ship, taken over by the Germans after she had been scuttled by the Italians. The twin deckhouses amidships are for electromagnetic housings for mine-clearing, termed *CAM-Anlagen*.

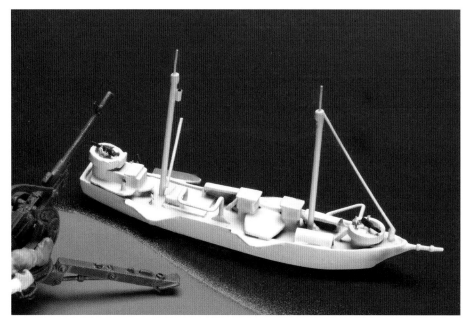

1/1250 Italian scratch-built schooner, with Argos photo-etched brass crew. The vessel is armed with two 76mm guns and two 8mm machine guns. A 20mm Mirliton Italian white metal Breda 20mm cannon and gunner is in the foreground, to simulate an AA gun on a cliff protecting Tripoli harbour, using forced perspective for this illusion, with the cliff then spray-painted brown.

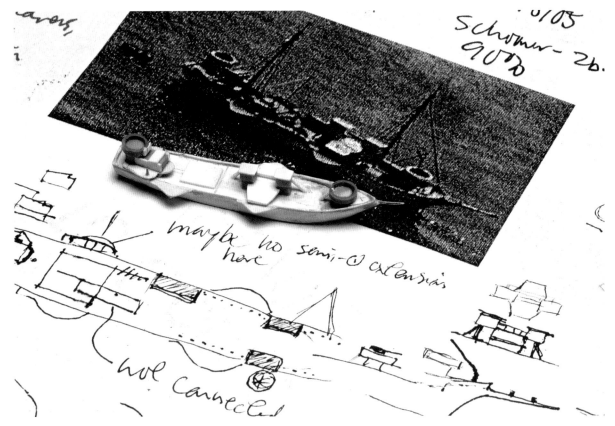

Partially-completed scratch-built schooner model, in 1/1250 scale, 5.7cm overall length. Model is laid on photocopy of not very sharp photograph used as reference for building the model, along with my interpretive sketches and building notes. For every complex scratch-build or conversion project, I always gather research materials, place them in a digital document, print them out and place them in three-ring notebooks, used as work logs for my ship model building. Techniques used and work times are carefully noted in these logs. Note variety of plastics used so far in construction of model. The forward tower structures probably comprised the *CAM-Anlagen* of Italian design, for countering magnetic mines. It is puzzling why this vessel has never appeared in any naval reference book, although there are some Internet images of possible comparable Italian vessels (helpfully sent to me via David Gregory).

Italian scratch-built schooner prior to painting and placing crew. A variety of materials were used. Turquoise is quick-print aluminium plate. Some structures are silver soldered. Ratlines are omitted, some features differ from photo and guns and machine guns are mounted. Hull is styrene-covered balsa wood, while the complex superstructure and fittings are a mix of different plastics and metals.

25

JAPANESE PICKET BOATS AND SEA TRUCKS

Japanese guard boats varied greatly in size, from about 18 to 3,943 GRT. The larger ones were usually steamers or auxiliary gunboats, while the smallest were fishing vessels/auxiliary mine-sweepers, best described as picket boats, which patrolled the perimeters of Japan's sea frontiers. Whatever their designation, over 200 such vessels were sunk by Allied aircraft and submarines; at least eighteen American submarines were sent on specific anti-picket-boat missions during 1944–5. In 1943 US aircraft sank two Japanese guard boats during one day in October, off Luzon and Rabaul, showing how such ships were widely utilised in the Pacific. Many examples can be seen in Harms' ONI CD (see Bibliography). Such craft had come to prominence in 1942 when two picket boats spotted the *Hornet* task force and radioed this information to the home islands, resulting in the B25s having to take off prematurely on their mission. The picket boats were sunk by cruiser gunfire. My scratch-built model is based on a bonito boat, broad-beamed and with distinctive partial sponsons, which were used as platforms by the fishermen when jigging for bonito. Boat sizes and gun armament varied for picket or guard ships.

Because of a lack of steel and the loss of so many merchant vessels due to Allied attacks, the building of wooden sea trucks, standardised in five classes from 100 to 500 tons, was started during 1943, probably largely in Japanese occupied territories, judging from photographs of building yards in such places. With almost no metal involved except the diesel engines (which gave a maximum speed of 8 knots) these ships were widely used for coastal cargo transport, as were landing barges and supply submarines later in the Pacific war. Many sea trucks had bowsprits, making them difficult to differentiate from wooden luggers. Harms (see Bibliography) is an excellent reference for these, while ONI publications N582 and 584 are good for larger Japanese

Typical bonito boat. Notice tapering hull, outboard sponsons, prominent bowsprit, and schooner rig.

Scratch-built hull of Japanese picket boat, based on bonito boat, seen in background as photocopy in 1/1250 scale, from ONI publication. Hull is made of balsa, styrene, lead and type metal, with aluminium quick-print plate bulwarks and sponsons, the latter being for the Japanese fishermen when jigging for bonito. Silver-soldered steel and brass bowsprit; note the broad beam.

Picket boat hull of balsa, with bulwark of aluminium strips. Front of hull is lead, with harder type metal inset to anchor soldered bowsprit of iron and brass, shown alongside hull before it was bent to shape. Hull was from an old model built decades ago, when balsa wood was my primary building medium.

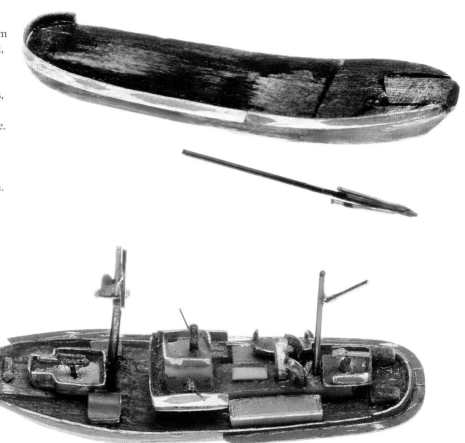

Scratch-built Japanese picket boat consisting of around fifty-six parts, including wood, plastic, lead, type alloy, aluminium, brass, copper, steel and silver solder. Constructing this model took around 39 hours spread over the course of 28 days, before painting. Getting the hull shape correct was the most difficult task, along with shaping and adhering the aluminium bulwarks and partial sponsons.

Finished Japanese picket boat, based primarily on a photo and painting in Gakken's *Imperial Army and Navy: Auxiliary Naval Vessels* and the *Hyuga Maru* in Harms' ONI CD-ROM. Upper masts were painted white to reduce visibility, and quilted, canvas anti-shrapnel coverings surrounded the bridge and pilot house. Argos photo-etched crew have been bent into more realistic poses. It is armed with one 8cm, one 25mm, two 13mm machine guns and two depth-charge racks. The overall length, including the bowsprit, is 3.05cm.

merchant ships, as is the Senpyosen website. Building models of picket boats and sea trucks takes a lot of guesswork on dimensions and details, as there is so little in the way of accurate information or plans available. Almost all model building of these vessels is based on interpretation of usually grainy WWII vintage b/w images from aerial or gun-camera photographs. But these ships played an important role for the Japanese Navy late in the conflict and so should be in the ship model collections of those with interest in the Pacific naval war.

Scratch-built Japanese steel sea truck based on a lead wargaming model by Trafalgar, which was clad by an aluminium sheet cut out of the outline of an actual sea truck. Hull and bridge filed to shape, then AA, funnel, lifeboat, hatches and booms installed, using iron, copper, brass wire, plastic sprue and sheet for hatches. The aluminium sheet was kept above deck level to provide bulwarks.

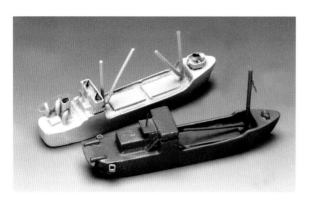

Scratch-built Japanese sea trucks, dark grey in wood with typical stern-mounted deckhouses. Light grey vessel is steel sea truck, armed with gun on bow and machine guns on top of bridge. Sea trucks were built in numerous local yards, so there is quite a lot of variation in their features. These models are 3.5cm in overall length.

Sea trucks and their subchaser escort *HB 17A* (1944) with false bow/stern waves, under attack by author's B24 extensively modified to PB4Y-2 or Privateer, with slightly smaller resin Privateer by commercial producer Vota Plane, 2.9cm and 2.6cm wingspans; these were heavily-armed US Navy patrol bombers of the late Pacific war.

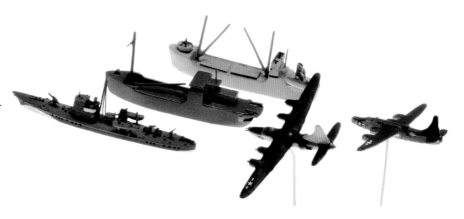

ABBREVIATIONS AND GLOSSARY

3D printed computer-controlled production of detailed models by layer upon layer polymerization of resins, often used as masters

AA anti-aircraft

air vents channels cut in mould to release air so molten metal can fill cavities

AMC armed merchant cruiser

anneal softening metal by heating, usually with a torch

APA USN attack transports

APD USN fast attack transports converted from destroyer escorts or flush-deck destroyers

Ar 196 German Kriegsmarine ship/shore-based floatplane

AV USN seaplane tender

B24 US long-range, four-engined bomber, used for maritime patrol and A/S

B25 US twin-engined Army, Marine medium bomber/strafer

B25H US twin-engined bomber with 75mm gun

BB battleship

Beaufighter British twin-engined fighter/bomber

'Betty' Japanese twin-engined Navy/Army bomber

BF 110 German two-seat day/night fighter

Black Cat USN black-painted Catalina used for night patrols

Bondo automotive filler useful for models

bonito boat Japanese fishing boat for jigging bonito, with sponsons

bowsprit spar extending forward from bow of ship

broadside number of guns that can be fired together along beam of warship

BV 138 German three-engine flying boat

C47 US twin-engined transport, widely used by US armed forces

CA/CL heavy/light cruiser

caique sailing vessels used in Aegean, often armed

calipers measuring tools, metric/Imperial

CAM-Anlagen German electro-magnetic mine detonating mechanism on *Sperrbrecher*

Carley float liferaft on many Allied ships

Catalina USN twin-engined maritime flying boat widely used by the Allies in multiple roles

catalyst an ingredient to speed up a chemical reaction

CinC former US producer of 1/2400 metal ship/aircraft models

CLAA anti-aircraft cruiser

Condor German four-engined maritime bomber

Convoy Rescue Ship ships outfitted to rescue torpedoed or disabled ships in a convoy

Corsair USN carrier-based Navy/Marine fighter/bomber, also used by British and other Commonwealth forces

corvette small class of escort vessel

crimp squashing a material to hold it in place

cruciform yards X-shaped yards, on German and French destroyers

cutter utility boat aboard ship, powered by oars or motor

CV/CVE aircraft carrier/escort carrier

cyano-acrylic glue fast acting, strong glue often used for model building, first developed to bind together wounds

Dauntless USN Navy carrier dive-bomber, successful ship killer, especially early in the Pacific war

dapping block metal block with various size round depressions; metal sheet hammered into these to make domes

DD/DE destroyer/destroyer escort

debubbled removing air bubbles from mould-materials during mould-making by a vacuum pump

DEM Defensively Equipped Merchant ship

depth-of-field how much of a photograph in focus

Devastator USN Navy carrier torpedo-bomber, replaced by Avenger

die-cast injecting molten metal, usually zinc alloys, into complex moulds for making models

drifter naval ship built on fishing boat for catching herring in drift net

'Emily' IJN four-engined flying boat, perhaps the best in WWII

Elco producer of USN 80ft PT boats

F4F/Wildcat/Martlet USN carrier fighter in early Pacific War, also used on British carriers and CVEs

F6F/Hellcat USN carrier fighter, late Pacific War, also used on British

carriers, most successful carrier fighter

FCS Fighter Catapult Ship

Fulmar British Navy two-seat carrier fighter, also used on FCS

gates channels cut into mould to permit molten metal to enter mould

gravity cast pouring molten metal into mould, using gravity to fill mould cavity

heat sink material surrounding mould to absorb heat of molten metal

He 111 German twin-engined bomber, often used as torpedo carrier against naval or merchant ships

He 115 German twin-engined multi-role seaplane

Helldiver USN Navy carrier dive-bomber, late Pacific War

Hilfskreuzer/**HSK** Kriegsmarine auxiliary cruisers, successful in early WWII, converted from merchant vessels such as fruit ships

HMCS His Majesty's Canadian Ship

HF/DF ('Huff Duff') high-frequency radio wave detector

ID identification, usually referring to models made for this purpose

IFF friend or foe detector on aircraft/ships

injection-moulded plastic models produced by intricate moulds fed with liquid plastic

IJN Imperial Japanese Navy

'Jake' Japanese ship-board and water-based reconnaissance floatplane

Ju 87/Stuka German dive-bomber

Ju 88 German twin-engined multi-role fighter/bomber

'Kate' Japanese carrier-based torpedo bomber

kamikaze Japanese aircraft ordered to crash into Allied warships

Kingfisher USN floatplane used on cruisers and battleships

KM Kriegsmarine or German Navy

latex rubber rubber in liquid form used for making moulds of model masters

LCF Landing Craft Flak

LCS(L) USN Landing Craft Support, Large

Liberator 1 early B24A modified by RAF Coastal Command as patrol/AS plane

lost-wax cast enveloping a wax model in

a plaster/clay mould, melting out the wax and pouring molten metal in resulting cavity

LSM(R) USN Landing Ship Medium, rocket carrying

LSS Landing Ship Support

lugger small, wooden fishing boat used for cargo by Japanese

MAC ship British/Dutch grain ship or tanker converted to carrier

MAD Cat Catalina with magnetometer for detecting submarines, armed with underwing rockets

MAL *Marine-Artillerie-Leichter* – German landing craft converted to gunboat

Mariner/PBM USN twin-engined maritime multi-role flying boat, also used by British Coastal Command

master detailed model used for creating moulds for casting

'Mavis' Japanese four-engined long-range reconnaissance seaplane

metallurgy study of how metals behave

minelayer ship designed or converted to lay mines

Mosquito British twin-engined high-speed bomber

'Nell' Japanese twin-engined bomber

OAL overall length of model

OBV Ocean Boarding Vessel

Ohka Japanese rocket-propelled suicide plane

Optivisor headband magnifying glasses

P38 Lightning US Army Air Force twin-engined long-range fighter, widely used in the Pacific war

paravane bow-mounted equipment for minesweeping

PC patrol craft

peened pin flattened to hold it in place

PGM USN patrol craft converted to gunboats

picket/guard/watch boat ship stationed outside a formation of ships or a geographical area as a warning unit

photo-etch chemically-etched steel or brass flat parts, used for models

piercing cutting out a space in material with a jeweller's saw

Plex Plexiglass, a transparent plastic used for aircraft windows, turrets and ship turrets

pom-pom British rapid fire 2pdr gun, single/multiple AA

port left-hand side of ship

Privateer/PB4Y-2 USN maritime patrol bomber, derived from B24

PT Patrol Torpedo boats, term used by USN, usually for Elco or Higgins motor torpedo boats

punch tool to cut out material

putty various liquid resins or plastic that set after exposure to air

Q-ship heavily-armed ships disguised as unarmed merchant ships, to combat U-boats

R-Boote Kriegsmarine minesweeper/escort

RAF Royal Air Force

ratlines climbing aids in rigging of sailing vessels similar to a rope ladder

resin cast models cast from liquid resins, instead of metal

RF radio frequency aboard ships

RN (British) Royal Navy

rotary tool hand-held battery or corded power tool that drive revolving tool bits, such as drills, burrs, rotary saws

RP rapid prototyping, via 3D printing

rpm revolutions per minute

RTV silicone room-temperature-vulcanizing silicone: a type of silicone rubber which cures at room temperature.

Rundwicklung type of electro-magnetic mechanism on German *sprerrbrecher* to detonate mines

runners passages that distribute molten metal from the sprue to gates or risers around the cavity inside a mould. Runners slow down and smooth out the flow of liquid metal.

S-Boote round-hulled German equivalent of US or British PTs or MTBS

sea trucks Japanese-built steel and wood boats of late Pacific war, used for cargo

schooner sailing vessel having a foremast and mainmast

scratch-building building models from raw materials

Siebel Ferry German pontoon ferry, often heavily armed

silicone polymers used for mould-making of model ships

Six/6pdr 57mm cannon used by RN

SMSC Society of Miniature Ship Collectors, US organization

soldering joining metal with a molten metal bond

SPBs/SPBR abbreviation for German mine destructor vessels

Sperrbrecher German vessel for mine destruction, also used as escort

spin/centrifugal cast casting molten metal into a spinning rubber mould, common way of producing ship models

sponsons structures overhanging hulls, used for mounting guns

sprued when a piece is ready for casting, with runners attached so molten metal can flow to it

SS submarine

starboard right-hand side of ship

strake protruding lateral plate on ship hull

Sunderland RN/Coastal Command four-engined flying boat, heavily armed, used for ocean patrol/A/S

swage to bend or shape metal by forging or squeezing

Swordfish/'Stringbag' RN single engine biplane used as torpedo bomber and A/S, carrier-based

'Taffy 3' USN task force of CVEs and light escorts that fought in battle of Leyte Gulf against much stronger Japanese force (abbreviation for Task Force 3)

TBF/TBM Avenger USN torpedo bomber/anti-submarine carrier plane, also used by British Fleet Air Arm

'Torbeau' British twin-engined torpedo bomber/fighter, heavily armed with machine guns, 20mm and rockets

trawler rugged, armed fishing boat used by all navies for patrol, escort and A/S

'Tsetse' British Mosquito with 57mm nose cannon, machine guns and rockets

TT torpedo tube(s)

Type 279 radar British early-warning radar, mounted on ships' masts

UK United Kingdom

USN United States Navy

vacuum cast using a vacuum to draw air out of a mould while pouring in the liquid metal

'Val' Japanese single-engine dive-bomber with spatted wheels, most successful ship-sinker in their navy

VES-Anlagen German electro-magnetic mine detonating mechanism on *Sperrbrecher*

Vorpostenboote German trawlers for patrol, escort, A/S

vulcanized using heat/pressure against a rubber mould and its metal master, to obtain the best mould detail

weathering fading and rusting of ship's paint due to the elements

whaler whale catcher ship converted to patrol/and A/S ship

white metal alloy of lead/tin for casting models; may contain other metals to affect temperature and casting properties

work hardening metal hardens or gets brittle when worked, like hammering or stretching wire

zareba shield to protect gun crews from blast, based upon African term for thorn shelter

Zero Japanese Navy and Army single-engine fighter, excelled until mid-Pacific war, also used as floatplane

RESOURCES

SHIP MODEL DEALERS: the following list of dealers is drawn from online sources and personal contact; those whom I have dealt with are in bold. I thank the SMSC website for much of the following information, although one should check to see if a dealer is still active. **1250 ships.com**, **Alnavco**, **Antics**, Arrowhead Miniatures, **Clydeside-flotilla.com**, Collectio Navilis, Galerie Maritim, **GHQ Models**, Konishi Metallic Model Collection, Legions IV Hire (still carries excellent CinC 1/2400 warships), Langton Miniatures, La Walu Modelle, Miniship europe, Mike's Modelle, Opatatus Berlin, **PT Dockyard**, **Paperlab.com, Rio Grande Model Shop**, Ships and More, Valiant Enterprises, **Waterline Ships Co.**, **L. Wiedling**. At regional or national meetings of the SMSC, I have bought many models, often at very reasonable prices. An added bonus is that one can know exactly the condition of the model.

SUPPLIES AND MATERIALS: Most supplies and materials ship modellers need can be found at hobby stores, or even craft stores but such merchandisers, especially hobby stores, are now hard to find. For plastic putty, I use Bondo, found in large tubes that will last for years, to be purchased from automotive stores. Similarly, a good source of large inexpensive spray paints are hardware stores in the form of automotive primers, which exist in a large range of greys suitable for naval ship models.

JEWELLERY SUPPLIERS FOR TOOLS: Rio Grande carries an extensive range of fine tools, many of which are suitable for the model builder. If used with care, good hand tools will last a life-time.

TOOLS: Most useful hand tools for ship models can be gotten at some bead stores, craft stores, the mail order/online store Micro-Mark (www.micromark.com) which has both tools and supplies useful to our community, or other jewellery suppliers in the US or those in your own country.

CRAFT STORES: In the United States, the chain of Michaels craft stores have a section for beaders and jewellers, which is good for some tools, thin wires in spools (cut off what is needed and stretch tight with two pliers, for straight and harder wire for models) and plastic boxes for holding small parts, glues, etc.

HARDWARE STORES: If you have an old-fashioned hardware store nearby, instead of big chain stores, they often have both useful tools and materials, like thin wire, otherwise not easily found.

PUBLICATIONS: With regards to magazines or journals that cover 1/1250 or 1/1200 ship/plane models, there is now only the occasional article in *Marine Modelling International* by Kevin Holmes, or the German journal *Hamburger Rundbrief*. *Warship International* and *Warship Journal* do cover warships, but not small scale models like ours. The SMSC website does provide an extensive list of publishers of maritime subjects and booksellers, although few of the latter send out periodic catalogues devoted to military/naval publications any longer. I have used Antheil Booksellers for years, obtaining books otherwise often difficult to find, as well as being the only bookstore in our small community, Cassidy's Books. Only used books are carried there, but due to the large number of retired veterans in this part of California, one can sometimes find scarce naval and other military books.

PHOTO-ETCH: I use Argos and Eduard photo-etched crew, Navalis radars and Gold Medal Model photo-etch products, but only Argos and Navalis are 1/1250, the others only make 1/700 for their smallest scales. Sometimes, one can adapt larger scales for use in our scale range. Micro-Mark does carry photo-etch kits.

DECALS: There are few good sources for decals for ships and planes, of which Navalis is one. The SMSC site discusses others, although some of these are subpar. Sometimes kits of larger scales will have decals adaptable to the small-scale ship builder. Micro-Mark offers kits for decal making, usually aimed at the model railroader. The message boards sometimes offer good sources for decals.

SALVAGE: An excellent source of materials for ship model building is what you can save from everyday items, like plastic closures for plastic bags, cocktail straws, thin wires that hold corks onto wine bottles, old credit cards, etc. One of my most useful modelling material is thin aluminium sheets from quick printing, although I am not sure if this type of printing plate is still used. Retaining sprues from plastic kits or metal castings provides good model shipbuilding material. Try to visualise how materials can be utilised.

FORUMS OR MESSAGE BOARDS AND ASSOCIATIONS: 1250 Scale Message Board for the US, Dockside Message Board for the UK, sammelhafen.de and Müncher Rundbrief for Germany; SMSC – Society of Miniature Ship Collectors for the US; Waterline Guide by Kelvin Holmes, courtesy of *Marine Modelling International* magazine (www.marinemodelmagazine.com). Additional message boards or forums: Steelnavy Message Board, Ship Model Forum, j-aircraft.com, German Navy Forum, Warships Projects Discussion Board, Marine Forum, Betasom.

AUCTION SITES Amazon and eBay both offer model ships on their auction sites, although it is often difficult to know the actual condition of a model, and bidding success can be tricky, due to various strategies used by experienced bidders. Often, prices on these sites are unrealistic, so one needs to have some idea of fair market prices. There are other auction sites that offer the occasional model or recognition models; these are sites that deal primarily in militaria. If in doubt about price or authenticity, ask an experienced collector.

BIBLIOGRAPHY

Albrecht, D. (ed) *Norman Bel Geddes Designs America.* (New York, Abrams, 2012)

Anonymous 'RAMB III—Rhenania model RHE-WI 9'. *Waterline International* IV (14) (1999)

— *Imperial Army and Navy: Auxiliary Naval Vessels.* (Tokyo, Gakken Research Institute, June 2002)

Achkasov, V.I. and N. B. Pavlovich *Soviet Naval Operations in the Great Patriotic War 1941-1945.* (Annapolis, Naval Institute Press, 1981)

Adcock, A. 1997 *Destroyer Escorts in Action.* (Carrollton, Squadron/Signal Publications, Warships number 11

— *WWII US Landing Craft in Action.* (Carrollton, Squadron/Signal Publications, Inc. 2003)

— *US Navy Ships Camouflage WWII: Destroyers and Destroyer Escorts.* (Carrollton, Squadron Signal Publications, 2008)

Ainsworth, M. *Warships in Miniature. A Guide to Naval Waterline Shipmodelling in 1:1200 scale.* (London, Conway Maritime Press, 2001)

Arndt, P. *Deutsche Sperrbrecher 1914-1945.* (Bonn, Bernard & Graefe Verlag, 2005)

Arnold, G.R. *Flush Deck Destroyers in World War Two.* Warship Perspectives. (New York, WR Press Inc. 2001)

Baggaley, P.M. 'Making miniature warships.' *Warship International* **29(2)** (1992)

Bagnasco, E. *Le Armi delle Navi Italiane nella seconda guerra mondiale.* (Parma, Ermanno Albertelli Editore, 2007)

— **and M. Brescia** *La mimetizzazione delle Navi Italiane 1940-1945. Italian Navy Camouflage 1940-1945.* (Parma, Ermanno Albertelli Editore, 2006)

— **and E. Cernuschi** *Le Navi da guerra Italiane 1940-1945. Italian warships of World War Two.* (Parma, Ermanno Albertelli Editore, 2005)

Baker III, A.D. *Allied Landing Craft of World War Two.* (Annapolis, Naval Institute Press, 1985)

Baker, R. et al. *Selected Papers on British Warship Design in World War II.* (London, Conway Maritime Press Ltd, 1983)

Bailey, R. H. et al. *Partisans and Guerrillas. World War II.* (Alexandria, VA, Time-Life Books, 1978)

Ball, D. L. *Fighting Amphibs. The LCS(L) in World War II.* (Williamsburg, Mill Neck Publications, 1997)

Barker, R. *Hurricats. The Fighters That Could Not Return.* (Gloucestershire, Tempus Publishing Ltd, 2000)

Beaver, P. *German Destroyers and Escorts.* (Tucson, Aztex Corporation, 1981)

Bergerud, E.M. *Fire in the Sky. The Air War in the South Pacific.* (Boulder, Westview Press, 2000)

Bird, A.D. *A Separate Little War. The Banff Coastal Command Strike Wing versus the Kriegsmarine and Luftwaffe 1944-1945.* (London, Grub Street, 2003)

Boesch, H. *Handelsschiffe im Kriegseinsatz.* (Oldenburg und Hamburg, Verlag Gerhard Stalling AG, 1975)

Botting, D. and eds of Time-Life *The U-boats.* The Seafarers series. (Chicago, Time-Life, 1979)

Bragadin, M.A. *The Italian Navy in World War II.* (Annapolis, Naval Institute Press, 1957)

Brennecke, J. *Gespenster Kreuzer HK 33. Hilfskreuzer Pinguin. Die erfolgreichste Kaperfahrt.* (Muenchen, Wilhelm Heyne Verlag, 1990)

—*Hilfskreuzer Thor. Hecht im Atlantik.* (Hamburg, Koehlers Verlagsgesellschaft mbH, 1998)

Breyer, S. *Die Deutsche Kriegsmarine 1939-1945.* (Friedberg, Podzun-Pallas Verlag, 1986)

Bridgland, T. *Waves of Hate. Naval Atrocities of the Second World War.* (Annapolis, Naval Institute Press, 2002)

Brown, D.K. (ed.) *The Design and Construction of British Warships 1939-1945. The Official Record. Landing Craft and Auxiliary Vessels.* (London,

Conway Maritime Press, 1996)

— *Nelson to Vanguard. Warship Design and Development 1923-1945.* (Annapolis, Naval Institute Press, 2000)

— *Atlantic Escorts. Ships, Weapons & Tactics in World War II.* (Annapolis, Naval Institute Press, 2007)

Brown, J. D. (edited by D. Hobbs) *Carrier Operations in World War II.* (Annapolis, Naval Institute Press, 2009)

Bruning Jr., J.R. *Ship Strike Pacific.* (St. Paul, Zenith Press, 2005)

Brzezinski, S. and P. Turalski *The American AA Cruiser USS Oakland.* (Wyszkow, Profile Morskie 83 , 2006)

Buckley, Jr., Captain R. J. *At Close Quarters. PT boat in the United States Navy.* (Washington, Naval History Division, 1962)

Campbell, C. *Air War Pacific. The Fight for Supremacy in the Far East: 1937 to 1945.* (New York, Crescent Books, 1990)

Campbell, J. *Naval Weapons of World War Two.* (London, Conway Maritime Press Ltd, 1985)

Carey, A.C. *We Flew Alone. United States Navy B-24 Squadrons in the Pacific. February 1943-September 1944.* (Atglen, Schiffer Military History, 2000)

— *Above an Angry Sea. United States Navy B-24 Liberator and PB4Y-2 Privateer. Operations in the Pacific October 1944 – August 1945.* (Atglen, Schiffer Military History, 2001)

Chesneau, R. (ed) *All the World's Fighting Ships 1922-1946.* (Annapolis, Naval Institute Press, 2006)

Cicco, A. De 'German Raiders – Le navi corsare tedesche.' *Waterline International* VI (19) (2001)

Cocker, M. *Aircraft-Carrying Ships of the Royal Navy.* (Stroud, The History Press, 2008)

Connelly, T. G. *US 110' Subchasers in Action.* (Carrollton, Squadron/Signal Publications , 2009)

Couhat, J. L. *French Warships of World War II.* (London, Ian Allan, 1971)

151

Cranwell, J. P. and S.A. Smiley *United States Navy Waterline Models and How to Build Them.* (New York, W.W. Norton and Co., Inc. 1947)

Cressman, R. *The Official Chronology of the U.S. Navy in World War II.* (Annapolis, Naval Institute Press, 1999)

Daley, C. *California and 1250 Models. The First Five Years 2004 to 2009.* (Claremont, Chris Daley Publishing, 2010)

Danner, H. *Kriegsfischkutter – KFK.* (Hamburg, Verlag E. S. Mittler & Sohn GmbH, 2001)

Darlington, R. and F. McKee *Three Princes Armed. Luxury Liners to Warships.* (Canada, self-published, 2008)

Date, J. C. *HMAS Sydney (11) Pt. 1: Sinking the Bartolomeo Colleoni 19 July 1940. Pt. 2: Tragic loss with HSK Kormoran 19 November 1941.* The Naval Historical Society of Australia Monograph (12) (1988)

— *German auxiliary cruisers of World Wars I (1914-1918) and II (1939-1945).* The Naval Historical Society of Australia Inc. Mongraph (68) (1999)

Davis, L. *B-24 Liberator in Action.* Aircraft number 80. (Carrolton, Squadron/Signal Publications, Inc. 1987)

Dickens, Captain P. *Night Action.* (New York, Bantam Books, 1974)

Dickson, R. *USS Juneau (CL 52).* (Kresgeville, The Floating Drydock, 1993)

Dorgeist, T., B. Tesapsides and R. Stenzel *Chronik der Küstenschutz-flottille Nordgriechenland 1941-1944.* (Münster, Edition Octopus, 2008)

Dorr, R. F. *B-24 Liberator Units of the Pacific War.* Osprey Combat Aircraft 11. (Oxford, Osprey Publishing, 1999)

Dorris, F. *Ship Models for the Military. US Manufacturers of Ship Models during the World Wars.* (Claremont, Chris Daley Publishing, 2010)

Downes, A.M. '"Q" ships in World War II - Service in HMS Botlea.' The Naval Historical Society of Australia Inc. Monograph (53) (1996)

Duffy, J.P. *Hitler's Secret Pirate Fleet. The Deadliest Ships of World War II.* (London, Praeger, 2001)

Duskin, G.L. and R. Segman *If the Gods are Good. The Epic Sacrifice of HMS Jervis Bay.* (Manchester, Crecy Publishing, 2005)

Elliot, P. *Allied Escort Ships of World War II. A Complete Survey.* (Annapolis, Naval Institute Press, 1977)

— *Allied Minesweeping in World War 2.* (Annapolis, Naval Institute Press, 1979)

Ethell, J. L. *Luftwaffe at War 4. Eagles over North Africa and the Mediterranean 1940-1943.* (London, Greenhill Books and Pennsylvania, Stackpole Books, 1997)

— **and W. M. Bodie** WW II *Pacific War Eagles. China/Pacific Aerial Conflict in Original Color.* (Fort Royal, Widewing Publications, 1997)

Fock, H. *Z-vor! Internationale Entwicklung und Kriegseinsätze von Zerstörern und Torpedobooten im Zweiten Weltkrieg 1940-1945.* (Hamburg, Koehlers Verlagsgesellschaft mbH, 2001)

Forrestel, Vice Admiral E.P., USN (Retired) *Admiral Raymond A. Spruance, USN. A Study in Command.* (Washington, D.C., 1966)

Forczyk, R. *German Commerce Raider vs British Cruiser.* (Oxford, Osprey Publishing , 2010)

Fraccaroli, A. *Italian Warships of World War II.* (London, Ian Allan, 1968)

— *Italian merchant armed cruisers in World War II. In:* Osborne, Dr. R. (ed) *Conversion for war.* (Cumbria, World Ship Society Monograph (6) 1983)

Freivogel, Dr. Z. 2001 *Deutsche Hilfskreuzer auf allen Meeren* (Teil 1). Marine-Arsenal 48: 1-32.

Friedman, N. *U.S. Cruisers. An Illustrated Design History.* (Annapolis, Naval Institute Press, 1984)

— *Naval Anti-Aircraft Guns and Gunnery.* (Annapolis, Naval Institute Press, 2013)

— *U.S. Battleships: An Illustrated Design History* (Annapolis, Naval Institute Press, 2016)

Fukui, S. *Japanese Naval Vessels at the End of World War II.* (Annapolis, Naval Institute Press, 1991)

Gibbs, J., P.C. Jumonville and J. Pauly Question 27/51 (W.I. No.3 (2014): 207. 'Condition of French Battleship Jean Bart on 8 November 1942.' *Warship International* 52 (3) (2015)

Giorgerini, G. and A. Nani *Almanacco storico delle Navi militari italiane 1861-1995.* (Roma, Ufficio Storico Della Marina Militare, 1996)

Góralski, W. and G. Nowak *Japanese Battleship Kongo. Super Drawings in 3D.* (Lublin, Kagero, 2008)

Greene, J. and A. Massignani *The Naval War in the Mediterranean 1940-1943.* (London, Chatham Publishing, 1998)

Griehl, M. *Airwar over the Atlantic. Lufftwaffe at war.* (Mechanicsburg, Stackpole Books, 2003)

Gröner, E., D. Jung und M. Maas *Die deutschen Kriegsschiffe 1815-1945. U-Boote, Hilfskreuzer, Minenschiffe, Netzleger und Sperrbrecher. Band 3.* (Koblenz, Bernard & Graefe Verlag, 1985)

— *Hafenbetriebsfahrzeuge (Teil II: Bagger, Bergungs-und Taucherfahrzeuge, Eisbrecher, Schlepper, Verkehrsfahrzeuge), Yachten und Aviso, Landungsverbände (Teil I Lotsen-und Seezeichenwesen). Band 6.* (Koblenz, Bernard & Graefe Verlag, 1990)

— *Landungsverbände (II): Landungsfahrzeuge i.e. S. (Teil 2), Landungsfähren, Landungsunterstützungsfahrzeuge, Transporter; Schiffe und Boote des Heeres, Schiffe und Boote der Seeflieger/Luftwaffe, Kolonialfahrzeuge. Band 7.* (Koblenz, Bernard & Graefe Verlag, 1990)

— *Die deutschen Kriegsschiffe 1815-1945. Flussfahrzeige, Ujäger, Vorpostenboote, Hilfsminensucher, Küstenschutzverbände (Teil 1). Band 8/1.* (Koblenz, Bernard & Graefe Verlag, 1993)

— *Die deutschen Kriegsschiffe 1815-1945. Vorpostenboote, Hilfsminensucher, Küstenschutzverbände (Teil 2), Kleinkampferbände, Beiboote. Band 8/2.* (Koblenz, Bernard & Graefe Verlag, 1993)

Guiglini, J. 'The 2400-toners of the French Navy.' *Warship International* XVIII(2) (1981)

Gunston, W. *Illustrated Encyclopedia of Combat Aircraft of World War II.* (New York, Bookthrift, Inc. 1978)

Hague, A. 'Q-Ships.' *In:* Osborne, Dr. R. (ed) *Conversion for War.* (Cumbria, World Ship Society Monograph (6) 1983)

— *Convoy Rescue Ships 1940-1945.* (Gravesend, World Ship Society 1998)

— *The Allied Convoy System 1939-1945. Its Organization, Defence and Operation.* (Annapolis, Naval Institute Press, 2000)

Harmon, J. S. *U.S.S. Cassin Young (DD-793). A Fletcher Class Destroyer.* (Missoula, Pictorial Histories Publishing Co, 1985)

Harms, N.E. *Merchant & Military Vessels of World War II Reviewed. Vol. I. A RE-presentation of ONI 208-J -Supplement 2. Far Eastern and ONI 223M - Merchant Ship Shapes.* CD-ROM. (Anaheim, Scale Specialties. 2000)

Hayden, S. *Wanderer.* (Dobbs Ferry, Sheridan House, Inc. 1998)

Hickey, L.J. *Warpath across the Pacific. The Illustrated History of the 345th Bombardment Group during World War II.* Eagles over the Pacific Vol. I (Boulder, International Research and Publishing Corporation, 1996)

Hodges, P. and N. Friedman *Destroyer Weapons of World War 2.* (Annapolis, Naval Institute Press, 1979)

Holmes, K. A guide to 1/1200 and 1/1250 waterline model ships. 5th issue, 2009 (Downloaded from MSM, www.collectableships.com)

Hoving, A. 'Restoration of two Dutch ship models with thoughts on ethics and practice.' *Nautical Research Journal* 43 (1) (1998)

Huan, C. *Les Sous-Marins Français 1918-1945.* (Bourg en Bresse, Marines Editions, ca. 1990)

Hutson, H. C. *Grimsby's Fighting Fleet. Trawlers and U-boats in the Second World War.* (Beverley, Hutton Press Ltd. 1990)

Inoguchi, R., Capt. and Cdr. T. Nakajima with R. Pineau *The Divine Wind. Japan's Kamikaze Force in World War II.* (Annapolis, Naval Institute Press, 1994)

Jablonski, E. *Airwar. An Illustrated History of Airpower in the Second World War.* (Garden City, Doubleday & Co. 1979)

Jacobs, P. 1990s (?) 'One to one hundred.' *Plastic Ship Modeler* 6/4, no. 24: 34.

— 1997 'One to one hundred.' *Plastic Ship Modeler* 4/2: 27.

— 2000 (?) 'One to one hundred.' *Plastic Ship Modeler* 7/1, no. 25: 30. [Note: a number of issues of this now defunct journal were undated]

— *Miniature Ship Models. A History and Collector's Guide.* (Annapolis, Naval Institute Press, 2008)

Jarski, A. and M. Skwiot *Akagi.* Encyklopedia Okrętów Wojennych Vol. 2. (Gdansk, AJ-Press, 2009)

Jentschura, H., D. Jung and P. Mickel *Warships of the Imperial Japanese Navy. 1869-1945.* (Annapolis, Naval Institute Press, 1982)

Jefferson, D. *Coastal Forces at War. The Royal Navy's 'Little Ships' in the Narrow Seas 1939-1945.* Second Edition. (Sparkford, Hynes Publishing, 2008)

Johnsen, F. A. (ed/publisher) 'Liberator Lore. Navy Liberators and Privateers, Stateside War Stories, Photo Gallery.' *Air Museum Journal* Vol. 4 (1989)

Johnston, M. *Corvettes Canada. Convoy veterans of WWII tell their true stories.* (Mississauga, John Wiley & Sons Canada Ltd. 2008)

Jordan, J. and R. Dumas *French Battleships 1922-1956.* (Annapolis, Naval Institute Press, 2009)

Jung, D., A. Abendroth, N. Kelling *Anstriche und Tarnanstriche der deutschen Kriegsmarine.* (München, Bernard & Graefe Verlag, 1977)

Kaplan, P. and J. Currie *Convoy. Merchant Sailors at War 1939-1945.* (London, Aurum Press Ltd, 1998)

Kemp, P. *Convoy! Drama in Arctic Waters.* (Edison, Castle Books, 2004)

Kenney, G.C. *General Kenney Reports. A Personal History of the Pacific War.* Air Force History & museums Program, 1997)

Kizu, T. (ed.) Auxiliary vessels of the Imperial Japanese Navy. (Tokyo, *Ships of the World* (522) 1997)

Kohl, H. *Fischdampfer und Walfangboote im Krieg.* (Hamburg, Verlag E.S. Mittler & Sohn GmbH, 2002)

Kugler, R. *Das Landungswesen in Deutschland seit 1900.* (Berlin, Oberbaum Verlag, 1989)

Lake, D. *Smoke and mirrors. Q-ships against U-boats in the First World War.* (Sutton Publishing, Stroud, 2006)

Lambert, J.W. *Bombs, torpedoes and kamikazes.* Air Combat Photo History Series Vol.2 (Stillwater, Specialty Press, 1997)

Le Masson, H. *The French Navy. Navies of the Second World War.* Vol. 2 (London, MacDonald, 1969)

Lengerer, H. 'Motor torpedo boats of the Imperial Japanese Navy. Part I.' *Warship International* XLIV (3) (2007)

Lenton, H.T. *German Surface Vessels 2. Navies of the Second World War.* (Garden City, Doubleday & Co., Inc. 1967)

— *American Fleet and Escort Destroyers. Navies of the Second World War.* Vol. 1 (Garden City, Doubleday & Co., Inc, 1971)

— *German Warships of the Second World War.* (New York, Arcs Publishing Co., Inc, 1976)

— **and J.J. Colledge** *Warships of World War II. Part four: Auxiliary fighting vessels.* (London, Ian Allen, 1962)

— *Warships of World War II. Part six: Trawlers.* (London, Ian Allan Ltd, 1963)

— *Warships of World War II. Part eight: Landing craft.* (London, Ian Allen Ltd, 1963)

Liu, R. K. '1/2400 scale ship models.' *Plastic Ship Modeler Quarterly* 1997/1 (1997)

— 'The historical bases of naval ship model scales.' *Waterline International* IV (13) (1999)

— 'Collecting naval ship models by theaters of operation.' *Waterline International* VI (20) (2002)

— 'AMCs and HSKs: Improvised warships of WWII'. Part one. *Waterline International* VIII (26) (2004)

— 'AMC E HSK (Incrociatori Ausiliari) ovvero le navi da guerra improvvisate durante la 2^Guerra Mondiale.' *Waterline International* VIII (26) (2004)

— 'AMCs and HSKs: Improvised Warships of WWII. Part two.' *Waterline International* VIII (27) (2004)

— 'AMC E HSK (Incrociatori Ausiliari) ovvero le navi da guerra improvvisate durante la 2^Guerra Mondiale. Secona parte.' *Waterline International* VIII (27) (2004d)

— 'Armed caiques and schooners of World War (II).' *Waterline International* IX (31) (2005)

— 'Caicchi e velieri armati della Second Guerra Mondiale.' *Waterline International* IX (31) (2005)

— *AMCs and HSKs: Allied and Axis Improvised Warships of World War II.* (San Marcos, Robert K. Liu, 2006)

— *Conversion for War. Mercantiles to warships in World War II.* (San Marcos, Robert K. Liu, 2009)

— *Naval Ship Models of World War II. Care, cleanup, repair, detailing, conversion and scratchbuilding of 1/1250 and 1/1200 ship and plane models of World War II.* (San Marcos, Robert K. Liu, 2010)

— *Naval Anti-Aircraft in World War II. Expressed via 1/1250 and 1/1200 ship and Plane Models.* (San Marcos, Robert K. Liu, 2014)

Lund, P. and H. Ludham *Trawlers Go to War.* (London, New English Library, 1971)

Lynch, T. G. 'Canada's Flowers. History of the corvettes of Canada 1939-1945.' Bennington, International Graphics Corporation, *Military Journal Special* 5 (1981)

Marcon, T. 'Gli incrociatori ausiliari della Regia Marina.' *Storia Militare* (165) (1997)

Maru eds. *Mechanisms of Japanese Destroyers.* (Tokyo, Kojinsha, 1999)

Meister, J. *Soviet Warships of the Second World War.* (New York, Arcs Publishing Co., Inc, 1977)

Miller, W. H., Jr. *Pictorial Encyclopedia of Ocean Liners, 1860-1994.* (New York, Dover Publications, Inc. 1995)

Morciano, M. *Classic Waterline Ship Models in the 1:1200/1250 scale.* (Rome, Waterline Italia, 2003)

Morison, S.L. (ed) *United States Naval Vessels. The official United States Navy reference manual prepared by the Division of Naval Intelligence 1 September 1945.* (Atglen, Sciffer Military History, 1996)

Moscinski, J. and S. Brzezinski *The British Antiaircraft Cruiser Delhi.* (Wyszkow, Profile Morski 40, 2001)

— *The British AA Cruiser HMS Colombo.* (Wyszkow, Profile Morski 48, 2002)

Muggenthaler, A. K. *German Raiders of World War II.* (Englewood Cliffs, Prentice-Hall, 1977)

Mussino, A. 'Brioni Class M.N. Barletta, Auxiliary Cruiser D 16—the new 1:1250 Barletta resin model (WI-R 01) and Delphis models resin kit 1:700.' *Waterline International* VII (23) (2003)

Naims, G. and L. Frädrich *Seekrieg im Ärmelkanal. Vorpostenboote an voderster Front.* (Hamburg, Verlag E. S.Mittler & Sohn GmbH, 2003)

Nesbit, Roy C. *The Armed Rovers. Beauforts & Beaufighters over the Mediterranean.* (Shrewsbury, Airlife Publishing Ltd, 2002)

O.N.I. *US Naval Vessels 1943.* (London, Arms and Armour Press, 1986)

— *Japanese Naval Vessels of World War Two, as seen by U.S. Naval Intelligence.* (Annapolis, U.S. Naval Institute Press, 1987

— O.N.I. 208 *Merchant Ship Recognition Manual, 1942.* (2002 – 2005)

O.N.I. 208 - J Japanese merchant ships recognition manual, 1942. History on CD-ROM N577.

— O.N.I. 208-J (revised) *Japanese Merchant Ships Recognition Manual, 1944.* O.N.I. 208 J (revised) Supplement No. 1 (May 1944). History on CD-ROM N582. (2002 – 2008)

O'Hara, V. P. *The U.S. Navy Against the Axis. Surface Combat 1941-1945.* (Annapolis, Naval Institute Press, 2007)

— *Struggle for the Middle Sea. The Great Navies at War in the Mediterranean Theater, 1940-1945.* (Annapolis, Naval Institute Press, 2009)

— *In Passage Perilous. Malta and the Convoy Battles of June 1942.* (Bloomington, Indiana University Press, 2013)

—, **W. D. Dickson and R. Worth** *On Seas Contested. The Seven Great Navies of the Second World War.* (Annapolis, Naval Institute Press, 2010)

Osborne, Dr. R. (ed) *Conversion for War.* Monograph (6). (Cumbria, World Ship Society, 1983)

—, **H. Spong and T. Grove** *Armed Merchant Cruisers 1878-1945.* (Cumbria, World Ship Society, 2007)

Parillo, M. P. *The Japanese Merchant Marine in World War II.* (Annapolis, Naval Institute Press, 1993)

Pope, D. *Flag 4. The Battle of Coastal Forces in the Mediterranean 1939-1945.* (London, Chatham Publishing, 1998)

Preston, A. and A. Raven *Flower class corvettes.* Man o' War 7. (London, Lionel Leventhal Ltd, 1982)

Price, A. *Aggressors. Patrol Aircraft vs Submarine.* Vol.4 (Charlottesville, Howell Press, 1991)

Ragnarsson, R. *US Navy PBY Catalina Units of the Atlantic War.* Osprey Combat Aircraft 65. (New York, Osprey Publishing Ltd, 2006)

Raven, A. *Camouflage Volume Three: Royal Navy 1943-1944.* Warship Perspectives. (New York, WR Press Inc. 2001)

Reminick, G. *Action in the South Atlantic. The sinking of the German raider Stier by the Liberty ship Stephen Hopkins.* (Palo Alto, The Glencannon Press, 2006)

Reynolds, L.C. *Motor Gunboat 658. The small boat war in the Mediterranean.* (London, Cassell Military Paperbacks, 2002)

Richards, B. *Secret Flotillas. Vol. II: Clandestine Sea Operations in the Mediterranean, North Africa and the Adriatic 1940-1944.* (London, Whitehall History Publishing in association with Frank Cass, 2004)

Rielly, R. L. *Mighty Midgets at War. The saga of the LCS (L) ships from Iwo Jima to Vietnam.* (Central Point, Hellgate Press, 2000)

— *Kamikazes, Corsairs, and Picket Ships. Okinawa, 1945.* (Philadelphia, Casemate, 2008)

Rohwer, J. *The Critical Convoy Battles of March 1943.* Annapolis, Naval Institute Press, 1977)

— *War at Sea 1939–1945.* London, Caxton Editions, 2001)

— and **G. Hummelchen** *Chronology of the War at Sea 1939-1945. The Naval History of World War Two.* (Annapolis, Naval Institute Press, 1992)

Romanoff Rubber Company, H. Mayer and J. Carter *The Art and Science of Centrifugal Casting.* (New York, Romanoff International Ltd. 1977)

Ronarc'h, J. P., Vice-Amiral *L'Évasion du Jean Bart Juin 1940.* (Paris, Flammarion, 1951)

Roscoe, T. *United States Destroyer Operations in World War II.* (Annapolis, Naval Institute Press, 1953)

Roskill, S.W. *White Ensign. The British Navy at War 1939-1945.* (Annapolis, United States Naval Institute, 1960)

Rottman, G. L. *Landing Craft, Infantry and Fire Support.* (New York, Osprey Publishing, 2009)

Scarborough, Capt. W.E. *PBY Catalina*

in action. Aircraft number 62. (Carrollton, Squadron/Signal Publications, Inc. 1983)

— *PBY Catalina Walk Around.* Walk around number 5. (Carrollton, Squadron/Signal Publications, Inc. 1995)

Scarpaci, W. *French Battleships 1933-1970. An Illustrated Technical Reference.* (Gardnerville, Art by Wayne, 2009)

— *Italian Battleships 1928-1957. An Illustrated Technical Reference.* (Gardnerville, Art by Wayne , 2009)

Schenk, P. *Kampf um die Ägäis. Die Kriegsmarine in Griechischen Gewässern 1941 - 1945. Für Randolph Kugler.* (Hamburg, Verlag E.S. Mittler & Sohn GmbH, 2000)

Schmalenbach, P. *A History of Auxiliary Cruisers of the German Navy. 1895-1945.* (Annapolis, Naval Institute Press, 1979)

Scutts, J. *Fletcher DDs in Action.* Warship No.8. Carrollton, Squadron/Signal Publications, 1995)

— *War in the Pacific. From the fall of Singapore to Japanese surrender.* (San Diego, Thunder Bay Press, 2000)

Sears, D. *At War with the Wind. The Epic Struggle with Japan's World War II Suicide Bombers.* (New York, Citadel Press, 2008)

Seligman, A. *War in the Islands. Undercover Operations in the Aegean 1942-4.* (Gloucestershire, Sutton Publishing Ltd, 1997)

Showell, J.P.M. *German Navy Handbook 1939-1945.* (Gloucestershire, Sutton Publishing Ltd, 2002)

— *Fuehrer Conferences on Naval Affairs 1939-1945.* (London, Chatham Publishing, 2005)

Silverstone, P.H. *U.S. Warships of World War II.* (New York, Doubleday & Co., Inc. 1970)

Skwiot, M. *Niemiecka artyleria okretowaˊ. German naval artillery.* Vol. II (Gdansk, A.J. Press, 2005)

Slader, J. *The Fourth Service. Merchantmen at War 1939-45.* (Dorset, New Guild, 1995)

Smith, Jr., M.J. *Mountaineer Battlewagon. U.S.S. West Virginia (BB-48).* (Charleston, Pictorial Histories Publishing Co. 1999)

Smith, P. C. *Hold the Narrow Sea. Naval Warfare in the English Channel 1939-1945.* (Annapolis, Naval Institute Press, 1984)

— *Pedestal. The Malta Convoy of August 1942.* (London, William Kimber, 1987)

— **and E. R. Walker** *War in the Aegean. The Campaign for the Eastern Mediterranean in WWII.* (Mechanicsburg, Stackpole Books, 2008)

Stearns, P. *Q-ships, Commerce Raiders and Convoys.* (Staplehurst, Spellmount, 2004)

Stehr, W.F.G. and S. Breyer 'Leichte und mittlere Artillerie auf deutschen Kriegsschiffen.' *Marine-Arsenal* Sonderheft Band 18 (1999)

Stern, R. C. *U.S. Battleships in Action. Part 1.* Warships No. 3 (Carrollton, Squadron/Signal Publications, 1980)

— *U.S. Battleships in Action. Part 2.* Warships No. 4 (Carrollton, Squadron/Signal Publications, 1984)

SSM Staff 'Warship Modeling. East European Style.' *Scale Ship Modeler* 9 (7) (1986)

Talbot-Booth, E.C. *What Ship Is That?* (New York, Didier, 1944)

— **(ed).** *Merchant Ships 1949-1950.* (New York, McGraw-Hill Book Company Inc, 1949)

Tesapsides, B. *Die Kriegsmarine in der Ägäis im II WK 1941-1944. Schiffe, Einheiten, Fp.Nr., Offiziere, Gefechte.* (Münster, Edition Octopus, 2008)

Thetford, O. *British Naval Aircraft since 1912.* (Annapolis, Naval Institute Press, 1991)

Toghill, G. *Royal Navy Trawlers. Part one: Admiralty trawlers.* (Liskeard, Cornwall, Maritime Books, 2003)

Tully, A. P. *Battle of Surigao Strait.* (Bloomington, Indiana University Press, 2009)

van Willigenburg, H. *Dutch Warships of World War II.* (Emmen, Lanasta. 2010)

von der Porten, E.P. 'Ship models go to war.' *Nautical Research Journal* 41 (1) (1996)

Walkowiak, T. F. *Destroyer Escorts of World War Two.* (Missoula, Pictorial Histories Publishing Co., Inc. 2003)

Watts, A. J. *Japanese Warships of World War II.* (London, Ian Allan, 1971)

Wegner, D. 'Lead corrosion in exhibition ship models.' *Nautical Research Journal* 43 (1) (1998)

White, D. F. *Bitter Ocean. The Battle of the Atlantic, 1939-1945.* (New York, Simon & Schuster, 2006)

Whitley, M. J. *Destroyers of World War Two. An International Encyclopedia.* (Annapolis, Naval Institute Press, 1988)

— *German Coastal Forces of World War Two.* (London, Arms and Armour Press, 1992)

— *Cruisers of World War Two. An International Encyclopaedia.* (Annapolis, Naval Institute Press, 1996)

Wiedling, P. *Wiedlings Schiffsmodell-Register. Teil I Kriegsschiffe.* (Grünwald, Wiedling, 2002)

— *Wiedlings Schiffsmodell-Register. Teil II Handelsschiffe.* (Grünwald, Wiedling, 2004)

— CD: *Lotse catalog; Wiedlings Schiffsmodell-Register. Teil I Kriegsschiffe;* 340 p. *Wiedlings Schiffsmodell-Register. Teil II Handelsschiffe:* 382 p. (Grünwald, Wiedling, 2004)

Williamson, G. *Kriegsmarine Coastal Forces.* (Oxford, Osprey Publishing, 2009)

Wilske, M. *Das deutsche Flugzeuträgerproject Graf Zeppelin entsteht.* (Berlin, edition Erich Gröner, 2019)

Winchester, J. (general ed.) *Aircraft of World War II. The Aviation Factfile.* (San Diego, Thunder Bay Press, 2004)

Winton, J. *Air Power at Sea 1939-1945.* (New York, Thomas Y. Crowell Co. 1976)

Wiper, S. *Imperial Japanese Navy Takao Class Cruisers.* Warship Pictorial 30. (Tucson, Classic Warships Publishing , 2008)

— *Kongo Class Battlecruisers.* ShipCraft 9 (Barnsley, Seaforth Publishing, 2008)

Wisniewski, P. and S. Brzezinski *The Japanese A.A. Cruiser Isuzu.* (Wyszkow, Profile Morski 55, 2003)

Worth, R. *Fleets of World War II.* (Cambridge, Da Capo Press, 2001)

Wright, M. *British and Commonwealth Warship Camouflage of WWII. Volume 1: Destroyers, Frigates, Escorts, Minesweepers, Coatal Warfare Craft, Submarines & Auxiliaries.* (Annapolis, Naval Institute Press, 2014)

— *British and Commonwealth Warship Camouflage of WWII. Volume 3:*

Cruisers, Minelayers and Armed Merchant Cruisers. (Barnsley, Seaforth Publishing, 2016)

Y'Blood, W. T. *Hunter-Killer. U.S. Escort Carriers in the Battle of the Atlantic.* (Bluejacket Books. Annapolis, Naval Institute Press, 2004)

Yenne, B. *Seaplanes & Flying Boats. A timeless collection from aviation's Golden Age.* (New York, BCL Press, 2003)

Zolandez, T. 'Ask Infoser. Comments and Corrections. Question 37/00 (W.I. No.1, (2008): 28): Effectiveness of Shipboard Anti-Aircraft Fire.' *Warship International* 46 (2) (2009)

Internet Sites:

Dutch armed merchant cruisers (of WWII). http://leden.tref.nl/~jviss000/Merchant.htm.

Paul Jacobs German armed merchant cruisers – a photo essay.

http://www.steelnavy.com/1250GermanRaiders.htm.

The Ondina battle. http://leden.tref.nl/~jviss000/battle_ondina.htm.

Brian Lee Massey The Canadian Military Heritage Project. WW2 The Canadian Navy. http://www.rootsweb.com/~canmil/ww2/ww2ship.htm.

Armed merchantmen. http://en.wikipedia.org/wiki/Armed_merchant_cruiser.

US Naval Armed Guard and WWII Merchant Marine. http://www.armed-guard.com.

John Asmussen *Hilfskreuzer.* http://www.Scharnhorst-class.dk/miscellaneous/hilfkreuzer/hilfskreuzer_introduction.htm.

Other Japanese Ship FAQs.www.j-aircraft.com/faq/other_japanese_ship.htm

The German Kriegsmarine. www.german-navy.de/kriegsmarine/ships/auxcruiser/orion/index.html

Society of Miniature Ship Collecters. www.smsc-home.org.

SS *Conte Verde.* https://en.wikipedia.org/wiki/SS_Cont_Verde

ww6.enjoy.ne.jp/~iwashige/soya.htm. (Japanese marus and auxiliaries, 5/20/08 via Mike Meyer)

www.dutchsubmarines.com (on Dutch submarine operations)

www.ifelix.co.uk (naval and land wargaming)

www.uboat.net/allies/warships/ship

www.en.wikipedia.org./wiki/USS_Tinosa_(SS-283)

www.sjwalks.interkriti.org/hisbox06.htm (on armed caïque)

www.wlb-stuttgart.de/seekrieg/bildnachweise/schiffe (all types of warships, including the *motorsegler*)

http://www.rogerlitwiller.com/2018/11/04/the-sacrifice-of-www.ss-beaverford-the-heroic-saga-of-the-canadian-pacific-railways-ship-with-teeth/

INDEX

Models of ships include the producer's name, while actual ships have only the vessel's name. Both are italicised.

INDEX

Models of ships include the producer's name, while actual ships have only the vessel's name. Both are italicised.